SAMURAI OF THE WEST

DOMINIQUE VENNER

SAMURAI OF THE WEST

A HANDBOOK FOR DISSIDENTS

FOREWORD BY ALAIN DE BENOIST

ARKTOS
LONDON 2025

ΛRKTOS

🌐 Arktos.com 📘 fb.com/Arktos ✈ 📷 arktosmedia ✖ arktosjournal

ISBN

978-1-917646-85-7 (Paperback)
978-1-917646-86-4 (Hardback)
978-1-917646-87-1 (Ebook)

Translation

Alexander Raynor

Editing

Jafe Arnold

Layout and Cover

Tor Westman

CONTENTS

TRANSLATOR'S NOTE

BEFORE STUDYING the history of the *Nouvelle Droite* (French New Right) became my *raison d'être*, I first became aware of Dominique Venner when the American media reported on his suicide at Notre-Dame Cathedral in Paris, which took place on May 21, 2013. According to reports from the American press, Venner took his life in protest of the recently passed same-sex marriage law in France (May 18, 2013). They hastily crafted a narrative that painted him as a vile, reactionary, homophobic, curmudgeonly, Catholic traditionalist, someone simply lashing out against the social progress of the modern world. But anyone familiar with Dominique Venner's life, work, and intellectual legacy knows that this caricature is a gross misrepresentation. Venner was not a Christian, nor was same-sex marriage the primary catalyst for his final act. As we've come to expect from the mainstream press, their portrayal served more to reinforce ideological narratives than to convey truth. Venner's admiration for Christian civilization was sincere, yet he stood outside the faith itself. However, Venner would not consider himself a pagan either, at least not in the same vein as someone like Jean Mabire, who would wear a Mjölnir necklace. Dominique once told his wife, Clotilde, "You don't resurrect a dead religion." With that said, much of Venner's worldview was informed by the epics of Homer. If one had to distill his identity into a single word, that word would be *European*. He was not merely a man born on the European continent — he was a man shaped by, and deeply devoted to, the civilizational essence of Europe.

Dominique Venner was born in Paris on April 16, 1935, the son of a modest architect. His mother died of tuberculosis when he was seven. The loss of his mother at such a young age instilled in him a stoic sensibility and a lifelong taste for solitude. After completing his baccalaureate and spending a brief period at the *École des Beaux-Arts*, Venner enlisted in the French army at the age of 18. His military career would prove pivotal.

He volunteered to fight in the Algerian War of Independence (1954–1962), a brutal conflict between France and Algerian nationalists seeking independence. The war not only ravaged Algeria, but also deeply divided French society, sparking protests and violence both in North Africa and in mainland France. Politically unstable, the Fourth Republic proved incapable of resolving the crisis, a failure that would ultimately catalyze radical political change in postwar France. Venner joined the 4th Battalion of *Chasseurs à pied* as a sergeant, serving in the rugged terrain near the Tunisian border and fighting against the *Front de libération nationale* (FLN) insurgents in what he later described as a "medieval little war." He carried with him a copy of Nietzsche's *Genealogy of Morals*, already turning to the thinkers who would shape his worldview. Decorated with the *Croix du Combattant*, he left Algeria in 1956, disillusioned not only by the brutality of the conflict, but also by what he saw as the political cowardice of the French state. This disillusionment radicalized him. Returning to civilian life, he plunged into the militant nationalist scene, becoming a key figure in *Jeune Nation*, a revolutionary group founded in 1949 and led by Pierre Sidos, which fused anti-communism with a visceral rejection of the postwar liberal order. *Jeune Nation* was known for its oftentimes violent activism and its iconography: the Celtic cross. Venner was not merely a participant, but one of the movement's most driven operatives, engaging in street battles, attacks on political targets, and eventually, plots against the French government during the Algerian crisis. *Jeune Nation* would become the most prominent French nationalist organization in the 1950s, reaching an estimated 3,000–4,000 members. One example of their activism was in protest of Soviet military intervention during the Hungarian Uprisings of 1956: *Jeune Nation* activists stormed the French Communist Party headquarters in Paris and set fire to the building.

Following the Algiers Putsch of May 1958 — a rebellion staged in Algiers by French military officers and *pied-noirs* (Europeans living in Algeria) who, convinced the French government was abandoning them, formed a Committee of Public Safety and demanded the return of Charles de Gaulle as a strong leader — the National Assembly yielded to pressure and granted de Gaulle extraordinary powers. Within weeks he became head of government, and by 1959 he had established the Fifth Republic with a new constitution. In the aftermath, the Minister of the Interior, Jules Moch, issued a decree dissolving *Jeune Nation*.

Venner continued his clandestine activism. He participated in *La semaine des barricades* ("The week of the barricades") of January 1960, when *pied-noirs* and French nationalists opposing Algerian independence erected barricades throughout Algiers, occupied government facilities, and expected military backing for their cause. When this support failed to materialize, violent clashes erupted between protesters and government forces, leaving numerous casualties. The uprising collapsed on February 1st, with mass arrests that extended even into mainland France, ensnaring sympathizers such as Jean-Marie Le Pen.

By April 1961, Venner's underground activities led to his arrest. His capture undermined his plot to storm the Élysée Palace — an audacious plan presumably intended to end de Gaulle's presidency by one means or another. Though Venner himself could not carry out such an attempt due to his arrest, de Gaulle was the target of repeated assassination plots during these years, most famously the Petit-Clamart attack of August 22, 1962, in which OAS conspirators under Lieutenant-Colonel Jean Bastien-Thiry nearly killed him and his wife. Bastien-Thiry was later executed by firing squad, the last such execution in France, and historians estimate that de Gaulle survived as many as 30 assassination attempts throughout his lifetime.

At the time of his arrest, Venner was meeting Pierre Sidos for lunch in a Parisian restaurant; Sidos managed to escape, but Venner was wounded and apprehended by police. He was sentenced to three years in prison for "recreating a disbanded league" and "compromising State security," ultimately serving 18 months in La Santé prison between 1961 and 1962. Contrary to later rumor, Venner was never a formal member of the *Organisation Armée Secrète* (OAS), though many of his former *Jeune Nation* comrades did join the organization.

It was during this imprisonment that Venner began to critically reassess the failure of French nationalism. Reflecting on the collapse of the French-Algerian cause and the impotence of the OAS, he concluded that violent activism alone, unanchored by serious doctrine, was doomed to fail. From this insight emerged his short but programmatic essay *Pour une critique positive* (1962), a seminal text that laid out the need for long-term, disciplined ideological work.[1] Drawing inspiration from Lenin's *What is to Be Done?*, Venner called for a new type of nationalist cadre: intellectually rigorous, historically grounded, and metapolitically aware.

This vision materialized in 1963 with the founding of *Europe-Action*, a movement and journal dedicated to renewing nationalist thought in Europe. Eschewing nostalgia and chauvinism, Venner and his collaborators — many drawn from the *Fédération des étudiants nationalistes* (FEN) (1960–1967), a student organization founded as a successor group to *Jeune Nation* — advocated for a racialized pan-European identity, grounded in biological realism, cultural continuity, and anti-egalitarian philosophy. He promoted the idea of Europe as a civilizational bloc unified by shared Indo-European heritage and threatened by immigration, communism, and liberalism.

Europe-Action functioned as both think tank and training ground, publishing works by emerging figures such as Alain de Benoist (under the pseudonym "Fabrice Laroche"), Jean Mabire, and Jean-Claude

---

1   Dominique Venner, *For a Positive Critique*, trans. Aodren Guillermou (London: Arktos, 2017).

Valla. It also issued publications glorifying anti-communist resistance movements and dissidents. Despite its militant imagery, the project was primarily intellectual: a strategic realignment rather than a call to arms. It can be said that *Europe-Action* was the precursor to the French New Right. Despite its short lifespan (1963–1966), *Europe-Action* would launch the political careers of many associated with the French nationalist scene, such as François Duprat and Pierre Bousquet, who would both go on to be founding members of the *Front national* (FN), now known as *Rassemblement national* (RN), which is the largest political party in France today.

Venner's role in this transition from street fighter to theorist marks a key moment in the genealogy of what would become the French New Right. While *Europe-Action* never attracted mass support, its ideas endured through GRECE (*Groupement de recherche et d'études pour la civilisation européenne*), founded in 1968, and through the metapolitical strategies that would shape radical right-wing thought in France for decades. Contrary to mainstream accounts, Venner was not a founding member of GRECE and never belonged to it formally. Instead, in 1968, he founded the short-lived *Institut d'études occidentales* (IEO). That same year, the upheavals of May '68 — mass student protests and labor strikes that briefly paralyzed the country — shook the French establishment and eroded de Gaulle's political authority, leading to his resignation the following year. Ironically, as Venner stepped back from political activism to focus on history, the political landscape around him was erupting with even greater intensity.

In the decades that followed, Venner withdrew from political activism and dedicated himself to historical writing. A self-taught historian, he produced acclaimed works on the Russian Civil War, the Waffen-SS, and the history of firearms and hunting. Venner wrote several books on contemporary history, starting with *Baltikum* (1974), about the German Freikorps that had been active between 1918 and 1923. He would later give this material a second look in *Histoire d'un fascisme allemand, 1918–1934* (1996), enriched by his correspondence with Ernst Jünger. Several other historical works would follow: *Le Blanc Soleil des vaincus* (1975) about the American Civil War; *Histoire de l'Armée rouge* (1981), which earned him the Prix Broquette-Gonin (literature) recognition from the Académie Française in 1981; *Le Coeur rebelle* (1994), a reflective, biographical work on his activism, and a significant milestone in his journey; *Gettysburg* (1995); *Histoire critique de la Résistance* (1995); *Les Blanc et les Rouges: Histoire de la guerre civile russe* (1997); *Histoire de la Collaboration* (2000); *Histoire du terrorisme* (2002); *De Gaulle, la grandeur et le néant* (2004). He also founded and directed two prominent history journals, *Enquête sur l'histoire* (1991–1999) and the *Nouvelle revue d'histoire* (2002–2017). His landmark book *Histoire et tradition des Européens* (2002) offered a sweeping vision of European identity as a civilizational continuity from Homer to the present. Shortly thereafter, Venner wrote another masterpiece, *Le Siècle de 1914* (2006), which explores the causes and consequences of the First World War as it pertains to European civilization in the 20th century. His final work, published before his death, *Le Choc de l'histoire* (2011), which was a series of interviews conducted with his wife, Clotilde Venner (under the pseudonym "Pauline Lecomte"), became the first of his historical and political works to be translated into English.[2]

Venner's worldview was shaped by a search for rootedness, tradition, and aesthetic heroism in a disenchanted age. He saw in Europe's pre-Christian mythos and warrior ethos a spiritual alternative to modern nihilism. In 2013, he ended his life in a dramatic act of protest at Notre-Dame Cathedral, leaving behind a final testament, *Un samouraï d'Occident*, published shortly after his death, urging Europeans to awaken to their forgotten heritage. One year later, following his death, at the summit of Mount Olympus, the Iliade Institute was formed. The Iliade Institute is a think tank dedicated to "long European memory," fulfilling the posthumous wishes of Dominique Venner. Today,

---

2   Dominique Venner, *The Shock of History: Religion, Memory, Identity*, trans. Charlie Wilson (London: Arktos, 2015).

the Iliade Institute serves as the torchbearer of Dominique Venner's legacy and the struggle to defend European civilization.

To better understand the true motivation behind Venner's final act, we have chosen to include his suicide note, "The Reasons for a Voluntary Death." In it, we see that Venner's self-sacrifice was not a narrow protest against a single law, but a final, symbolic gesture to become a rallying cry against what he saw as the slow but systematic annihilation of European identity. This protest was aimed squarely at what has since been named "The Great Replacement," a term coined by the French writer Renaud Camus to describe the demographic and cultural displacement of white European peoples through mass immigration and the ideological dismantling of national traditions. Though the ruling class and their media organs scoff at the concept and dismiss it as a paranoid conspiracy theory, the reality can no longer be denied. One need only walk through the streets of cities like Paris, London, Rome, or New York City to see the transformation with one's own eyes. The very same elites who insist that replacement is a myth also celebrate the coming minority status of native Europeans in their homelands, a contradiction that can only be reconciled through the alchemy of Orwellian doublespeak. Venner's death was not an act of despair, but of defiance. It was a message to those of us still living: remember who you are, and fight for what remains of our civilization before it is extinguished forever.

Dominique Venner embodied the "warrior poet" archetype in the most literal sense, a man who lived by the sword before devoting himself to the pen, yet who never relinquished the discipline, honor, and sense of destiny forged in battle. His service in Algeria, marked by physical courage and a clear-eyed view of war's brutal truths, informed a lifetime of writing that blended historical erudition with a stoic and martial prose style. For Venner, the true warrior is also a guardian of memory, a craftsman of words as much as of deeds, seeking beauty and meaning amid the harsh realities of history. Like the Homeric heroes he revered, he saw life as a field of action where courage, loyalty, and the pursuit of excellence could ennoble existence, and where the written word could preserve the spirit of that struggle for generations to come.

Recently, I was rereading Guillaume Faye's book, *Why We Fight*.[3] When it was initially published back in 2001, Faye proclaimed that if European people do not wake up from their slumber in the next 20 years, then all will be lost. It was apparent even then that if Europeans did not act soon, it would become impossible to salvage our civilization. His warning was not just prophetic; it was a final plea to a people on the brink of cultural and demographic destruction. In the past decade, I would like to think that we have heeded the final call of Dominique Venner, as shortly after his death, the Western world was set ablaze. Populist movements and young white Europeans are in revolt all over the world. What once seemed like isolated voices of dissent have now become a chorus of defiance. The counter-offensive for the survival of European civilization has begun. The cavalry has arrived. Europeans have awakened. But now that the awakening has begun, the question remains: will we have the strength and unity to see this battle through to its end? The answer is that we must, because there is no other option. May the "prayers and hymns" of this breviary serve you well in the struggle.

I want to thank my friend Alain de Benoist for providing his foreword and eulogy. I want to thank the French publishing house, La Nouvelle Librairie, for providing Arktos Media with the translation rights. Finally, I would like to thank the Venner family, particularly Clotilde and Guillaume Venner, for their collaboration in this project to make the works of Dominique Venner known to the English-speaking world.

ALEXANDER RAYNOR
August 8, 2025

---

3   Guillaume Faye, *Why We Fight: Manifesto of the European Renaissance* (London: Arktos, 2011/2025).

FOREWORD

BY ALAIN DE BENOIST

ONE CANNOT approach *Samurai of the West* as one does other books. When one reads a sentence like "Only suffered death has no meaning. Willed, it has the meaning one gives it, even when it is without practical utility," or "It is here and now that our destiny is played out until the last second. And this ultimate second is as important as the rest of life. It is by deciding for oneself, by truly wanting one's destiny, that one is victorious over nothingness" — when reading this, it is difficult not to feel one's hands tremble.

Dominique Venner completed writing this book "on the Winter Solstice" of 2012. He knew at that time — and had known for a long while — that he would take his own life. He died by suicide in Paris on May 21st, 2013; we know where and how. His final book, published a few weeks later, is indeed a testament. This voluntary death, of which François Bousquet wrote that it was "long contemplated, meticulously prepared and serenely carried out" and "bears within it the nobility of soul that marked every stage of his life" — this death is, of course, what sheds light on and gives full meaning to his book.

Samurai of the West is a simple book, in the best sense of the word — one guided by a "clear line," a line that might also be called matinal or auroral, because it reveals truths. Truth is ultimately always very simple. The complications begin only when one has to argue. Dominique Venner was not an intellectual, nor strictly speaking a theorist. (For both good and bad reasons, he had little fondness for intellectuals!) Nevertheless, his essay reaches the core of things — indeed, the very essence. One understands why when reading the words of this unreserved admirer of Homeric poems — "those sacred poems tell us what we were in our dawn, like no others" — who writes that "Homer shows but does not explain, does not conceptualize." Such is the path taken by Venner. To present and make understandable his worldview, he, too, shows. He brings to vision, and through that, to mind, what pertains to the truth of history, the truth of man, and the truth of the world.

This book aims to present a worldview. A structured one. Venner says: "the first principle of Stoicism is coherence" (the second being "indifference to indifferent things"). His worldview is likewise entirely coherent. It emphasizes two axes: man's relationship with nature and the ethical models that allow man to give the best of himself. Most of this book, which weaves together material from various texts published in recent years in a way that highlights their coherence, is devoted to these two themes.

First, the beauty of Nature — that Nature which, as Heraclitus said, "loves to hide," long desacralized, yet always a source of refuge. "In absolute rupture with ancient wisdom," Venner writes, "the reason of the Moderns, Christian or atheist, has sought to do away with the enchantment of Nature along with the perception of necessary limits and the tragic sentiment of life cultivated ever since Homer." He explains how to return to it in a way reminiscent of the "retreat into the forests" that Ernst Jünger evoked in *The Forest Passage.*

And the bearing? "It means being one's own norm through fidelity to a superior norm. To hold to oneself in the face of nothingness. To be watchful so as to never 'recover' from one's youth. To prefer to put the world against oneself rather than to grovel before it." Venner reviews some of the "masters of bearing" familiar to him: the Homeric heroes, to whom he devotes some of his finest pages; the ancient Romans, whose lives were centered around *gravitas*, *virtus*, and *dignitas*; the Stoics, who "made suicide the philosophical act par excellence, a human privilege refused to the gods"; and finally, the samurai.

The book's cover features Dürer's famous engraving, *The Knight, Death and the Devil* (1513). "Dürer's solitary Knight, with an ironic smile on his lips, rides on, indifferent and calm. To the Devil, he does not even cast a glance." Dominique Venner clearly felt himself a brother to this great rebel who has endured through time and still speaks to us. Yet, he who thought that great civilizations are "different planets" also did not hesitate to present himself as a "samurai of the West," an adherent to the precepts of Bushido. One chapter of his book even proposes a "detour through Japan, an example of complete otherness compared to Europe."

"To exist is to fight what denies me," says Dominique Venner again. From the programmed invasion of our cities to the deliberate erasure of European memory, page after page, he continues to rail against what denies him. He challenges the "metaphysics of the unlimited," that excess (*hybris*) by which man has sought to master the world, confusing "more" with "better." "If Europeans have been able to accept the unthinkable for so long," he also writes, "it is because they have been destroyed from within by a very ancient culture of guilt and submission," and he proposes to oppose to this culture an ethic of honor: "I wish that in the future, from the bell tower of my village, as well as at those of our cathedrals, one will continue to hear the soothing chiming of bells. But I wish even more that the invocations heard under their vaults change. I wish that one ceases to implore pardon and pity and instead calls for vigor, dignity, and energy."

Dominique Venner claimed tradition, a term he defined in an uncommon way: "Tradition is the source of founding energies. It is the origin. And origin precedes beginning [...] Tradition is not the past, but on the contrary, that which does not pass and which always returns under different forms." It is by embodying tradition that Antigone stands against Creon, in the name of an immemorial legitimacy opposed to the legality of established disorder. "The rebel is in intimate relationship with legitimacy. He defines himself against what he perceives as illegitimate."

This is also why Venner rejected all historical fatalism. Those who knew him know how foreign negative discourse, personal attacks, and gossip were to him. Just as alien to him were those prophets of doom who proclaim inevitable decline. If he addresses a Europe "gone dormant," it is with the certainty that it will awaken. Martin Heidegger wrote that man is inexhaustible, in the sense that he always holds more in reserve than he shows: "There is always a provision of being." Venner simply says: "History is the realm of the unexpected." Thus, through his Roman gesture, he sought to deliver a message of protest ("I confess my disgust for the self-satisfied imposture of the powerful and powerless lords of our decadence"), but also one of foundation — that is, of will and hope — of a "reasoned and argued hope," as Bruno de Cessole wrote.

This "breviary" is neither a little catechism nor a recipe book (even if the author offers some advice "for existing and transmitting"). It is more like a compass. It is also an outstretched hand to lead us to the peaks, where the air is crisper, where forms become clearer, where panoramas reveal themselves and stakes become visible. It is an invitation to become who we are. And it is once again from Homer — of whom the Ancients said he was "the beginning, the middle, and the end" — that Dominique Venner draws this triad, which resounds like a directive: "Nature as foundation, excellence as goal, beauty as horizon."

Coming to history through critical observation of the present, becoming a "meditative historian" after having been a fighter, this man, "who offered a curious mix of tempered steel and velvet, of coldness and incandescence, of rigidity and elegance" (François Bousquet, again) has, through his death, become a figure of French history — a "distinguished man" in the sense of Plutarch. The historian is now part of history. Read his testament.

ALAIN DE BENOIST

PROLOGUE

I F THERE remained in me any reserve of compassion, I might pity the immigrants from Black Africa, the Maghreb, Turkey, or the Indian subcontinent who have been imported en masse with the aim of breaking the wages of European workers. A sordid goal associated with the infamous and perverse project of denaturing Europe through population replacement. In their trials, immigrants nonetheless find to their advantage public aid, charitable actions, the support of clan solidarities, and the moral succor that can be brought to them by returning to Islam, the religion of their homeland.[1]

The fate of the French who are called "*de souche*" [of native stock], those who, in the suburbs, are called the "Gauls," seems to me far more pitiful and desperate. And I know it is the same everywhere across today's disfigured Europe. It is therefore for these "native stock" Europeans that I reserve my compassion. No one ever speaks of them and their distress, except, in veiled fashion, when a riot forces the media to emerge from their silence for a moment. Thus, as for one such exceptional case, we have their account of a French woman who has been surviving for 30 years in La Courneuve (in the Cité des 4000), whose anonymity I will respect: Catherine C.[2]

This account has the value of an example. The time that has passed takes nothing away from its dark reality. It has only made it worse.

---

1   I am not pleading in favor of Islam. I am recording a fact.

2   Account by Marion Van Renterghem in *Le Monde* (November 12, 2005). This investigation followed the riots of November 2, 2005. All quotes come from this article.

Being a Minority in One's Own Home...

The setting, first of all. In front of her home, an empty parking lot covered with ashes from which emerge some half-charred trees, vestiges of previous riots. Shortly before, about 20 cars were burning under her windows. A scooter without an exhaust pipe circles with a hellish noise. No matter the date. This is part of the daily life of the last Gauls who have been unable to flee the suburbs of immigration. The media align themselves with the general directive not to speak of it. Sometimes, however, we do speak of it, such as here, when millions of euros go up in smoke and a little blood begins to flow.

"At the heart of the Cité des 4000, her neat little apartment contrasts the broken-down hall and the dirty and gloomy landscape of 'Balzac.'" For those who don't know, "Balzac" is a gigantic housing block, Catherine C.'s only horizon. And what about her? "A small elegant lady with very blue eyes, past 40, who well conceals her weariness with life and limits her outings to the bare minimum." In this sinister suburb, she has maintained her world, her "neat apartment" and elegance about her. Yet, life has not been kind to her. Born in Paris, her father put her to work in a factory at 16 to earn her living. She ran away, met her ex-husband, and became pregnant. She has done everything: cashier, cleaning lady, leaflet distributor, ironer. She has raised her five children, two girls and three boys, aged 19 to 28, whom she strives to hold with a firm hand.

Catherine no longer votes. She has been disappointed by the socialists and doesn't like the right, "but she could find herself with the extreme right," according to the journalist. She says she's had enough "of not speaking with anyone, of passing veiled women who don't look at her, of hearing the Quran blasting from cassettes, of being looked at strangely if she smokes during Ramadan."

Before, in the past, it was different. She used to go drink tea with her Algerian neighbor. Everyone got along well. "Now," she says, "I feel completely isolated. I am a very small minority. It's difficult to become a minority in your own home, you know."

These words spin around in my head. I feel flooded with sadness, powerlessness, and also admiration for this abandoned woman who, despite everything, stands upright.

"I am Catholic," she continues, "my companion is Jewish, my children's friends are Muslims. What is new is that the French of foreign origin are withdrawing into their origin, they no longer feel French. And I, French, feel bad." She feels all the more unhappy that her eldest son, 25 years old, has converted to Islam. "I take it very badly," she says, "it makes me sick." This son reproaches her for not being veiled.

"Even my sons are of a different culture than me. For them, being French no longer means anything. They no longer have a nationality, they identify vaguely with a religion, the one that is in the majority. They observe the gestures of Islam, the Muslim way of being and speaking, they are proud to belong to the majority. They don't want to be French, they would like to be blacks and *beurs* [North African Arabs] like everyone else, but they don't behave like Muslims. So many incoherent things…"

What can Catherine C., a little abandoned French woman, do? Nothing more than what she does with what she hasn't been given. One can admire that she hasn't gone off the deep end.

I think of her while writing these lines. I have thought of her for a long time.[3] I think of all the Catherine C.'s, these little abandoned French women. And a violent anger grips me.

I think of those who have manufactured this hopeless destiny for her and those from whom no gesture, no word is extended to her to prove to her that she is not alone and that we are fighting for her and her children. And to restore her only wealth: her pride, even alone and isolated, of being a French woman, a "Gaul" as they say, vested with

---

3   I had written this text in the heat of the moment, on the morning of December 10, 2005, after a night of torment. This torment has not ceased.

an entire heritage of ancient grandeur and unique beauty that no one, ever, will be able to steal from her.

The Knight, Death and the Devil

And there you have it: almost everything has been said about what revolts me more than anything else today, what makes me a rebel.

I'll immediately add that I have many other motives for revolt and rebellion in this world that has been manufactured for us — a world of sex, fun, and money. I confess my disgust for the self-satisfied imposture of the powerful and powerless lords of our decadence, corrupted to the bone, enslaved to the true powers and the new mafias. Yes, the arrogant and pathetic lords of the media and advertising, of religions, politics, and finance inspire more contempt than true revolt in me. To revolt would be to recognize in them a substance they lack. In the past, I revolted against a man whose politics seemed harmful to me, but this character, as hateful as he seemed to me at the time, had true greatness.[4] Today, faced with these pretentious and malicious dwarfs, I am a rebel. In plain language, I don't "go along." It has been a very long time since I believed in honeyed and moralizing speeches, screens for devalued schemes.

By contrast and distance, I feel in harmony with a great rebel who has traversed time and whom no one thinks of, but who is, nevertheless, the model par excellence. Dürer's *Knight*.

The Knight, Death and the Devil... The admirable engraving by Albrecht Dürer from 1513. The brilliant artist, who elsewhere executed on commission so many edifying religious works, shows here a confounding and audaciously provocative freedom... In those times, it was not good to ironize about Death and the Devil, the terror of good people and others, maintained by those who profited from it.

---

4   On this point of ancient history, I refer the reader to my essay *De Gaulle. La grandeur et le néant* (Le Rocher, 2004).

But he, Dürer's solitary Knight, with an ironic smile on his lips, rides on, indifferent and calm. To the Devil, he does not even cast a glance. Yet this scarecrow is reputed to be formidable. The terror of the era, as so many dances of death and purchases of indulgences remind us, the Devil lies waiting in ambush to seize the deceased and throw them into the eternal braziers of Hell. The Knight mocks this and disdains this specter, which Dürer wanted to render ridiculous. Death, he knows it. He knows well that it is at the end of the road. And so? What can it do to him, despite its brandished hourglass to recall the inexorable flow of life? Eternalized by the engraving, the Knight will live forever in our imagination beyond time. Solitary, at the firm pace of his steed, sword at his side, the most famous rebel of Western art rides toward his destiny among the woods and our thoughts, without fear or supplication. An incarnation of an eternal figure in this part of the world called Europe.[5]

The image of the stoic knight has often accompanied me in my revolts. It is true that I am a rebellious heart and that I have not ceased to rebel against encroaching ugliness, against baseness promoted as virtue, against lies elevated to the rank of truths. I have not ceased to rebel against those who, before our eyes, have wanted the death of Europe, of the civilization, people, and power without which I would be nothing. My life has partly merged with an era of regression for the French and Europeans, precipitated by the catastrophes of the Century of 1914, the aftermath of the Second World War, the Algerian War, which anticipated American globalization. Despite the boastful illusions maintained in France and elsewhere, it was already clear to the very young man I was that the two hegemonic powers united at Yalta in 1945, America and Stalinist Russia, had wrested from Europeans the conduct of their destiny, which reverberated in their daily life and

---

5   A dissident of the 20th century, the writer Jean Cau devoted one of his most beautiful essays to him, *Le Chevalier, la Mort et le Diable* (éditions de la Table Ronde, 1977). Facing Death, he imagines these words in the Knight's mouth: "I have been dreamed and you can do nothing against the dream of men."

their representations. This has amplified beyond 1990, after the end of the USSR, when the United States, having become the hyperpower, imposed its financial globalization on other nations and peoples, transforming them into consumers of useless and disposable products.

A Culture of Self-Hatred

But, in reflecting on this great reversal that has accompanied settler immigration and the Islamic conquest of Europe, I have come to the conclusion that if Europeans have been able to accept the unthinkable for so long, it is because they have been destroyed from within by a very ancient culture of guilt and compassion. It is also because they have been made to feel guilty in the name of sins that are constantly hammered into their heads. Battalions of academics, archaeologists, linguists, epistemologists, and historians of various periods have worked relentlessly to demonstrate that France and Europe are guilty of everything and are nothing. They are not even all mercenaries, they are often "useful idiots" as the Stalinists of old said with contempt to qualify the celebrities they manipulated for the benefit of their propaganda.

A typical example of this perversion was given to us in 2008 with the publication of the scholarly work of a young academic, Sylvain Gouguenheim, professor of medieval history at the École normale supérieure in Lyon.[6] Against the established idea that the medieval West discovered Greek knowledge only from Arabic translations, Sylvain Gouguenheim showed through a large number of facts that Europe had always maintained contact with the Greek world, notably thanks to Byzantium. He revealed among other things that the abbey of Mont-Saint-Michel had been an active center of Aristotle translations from the 12th century. By good fortune or misfortune for its author, Sylvain Gouguenheim's book was the subject of a laudatory article in

---

6   Sylvain Gouguenheim, *Aristote au Mont-Saint-Michel. Les racines grecques de l'Europe chrétienne* (Le Seuil, 2008).

Le Monde of April 4, 2008, under a well-known signature. This fact could not go unnoticed. It aroused an enormous mobilization of intellectual circles predominantly hostile, by choice or mimicry, to any European rootedness. From April 25, *Le Monde* reported "the emotion of part of the university community." About 40 names followed. This was the beginning of a veritable "witch hunt" aimed at expelling Gouguenheim from the University.

On April 28, an appeal was launched by two hundred "teachers, researchers, staff, auditors, students and former students" of the ENS of Lyon where Sylvain Gouguenheim taught. This Soviet "collective" demanded an investigation, asserting that the incriminated book "served as ammunition for xenophobic and Islamophobic groups." The school administration announced that it would create a committee of experts to "evaluate what follow-up to give." And so it was. An extravagant procedure! Gouguenheim had committed no other fault than infringing upon the intellectual fashion of the moment. On April 30, the newspaper *Libération* gave the floor to 56 "researchers" who reproached Gouguenheim's book for a presupposition "with unacceptable political connotations." This was only the beginning. There was, however, a call for calm from the great medievalist Jacques Le Goff, who said he was "outraged by the attacks" against his young colleague. This undoubtedly saved the latter from complete destruction.

One wondered, naively: what had led various "collectives" to enter into war against Sylvain Gouguenheim's book? Why such hatred? The answer was provided in 2009 by a collective work published by a major publisher (Fayard) under the title *Les Grecs, les Arabes et nous. Enquête sur l'islamophobie savante* ("The Greeks, the Arabs, and Us: An Inquiry into Scholarly Islamophobia"). This indigestible pamphlet of 370 pages had been produced under the direction of four authors, including Alain de Libera. On page 8, these authors revealed what had motivated them. According to them, "*Aristote au Mont-Saint-Michel*" was part of "a will to definitively 'liquidate' May '68." The relation between

Sylvain Gouguenheim's book and the supposed "liquidation" of May '68 — here was something that was not self-evident!

Despite the absurdity to it, this justification nevertheless revealed the motivations of Gouguenheim's attackers. Beyond their frenzied Islamophilia, they showed themselves for what they were. Instead of academics in love with truth, one discovered ex- or neo-'68-ers' tinged with Trotskyism, pursuing an old ideological battle under the trappings of support for Muslim immigration. A battle that led them to castigate several great medievalists and to attack even, *post mortem*, Fernand Braudel and his concept of civilization.

Europe in Dormition

The inculcation of guilt in Europeans has facilitated the masked invasion of their territories and the "great replacement" of their populations, something that has no precedent in the past. And if it has been possible to impose this monstrous enterprise, whose consequences will be paid dearly in the long term, it is certainly because of the complicity of perverse and decadent elites, but above all because Europeans, unlike other peoples, are devoid of memory of their identity and consciousness of what they are. A very deep-rooted, old foundation of universalist culture, religious or secular, predisposed them to undergo invasion as something normal, which the ruling oligarchies themselves have proclaimed desirable and beneficial.

Such is the masked reality that cannot be separated from a major historical fact. Since the end of the two world wars and their debauchery of violence, Europe has "entered into dormition," despite some boastful speeches.[7]

This state of "dormition" is the consequence of the excesses of murderous and fratricidal fury perpetrated between 1914 and 1945. It is also the gift handed to Europeans by the United States and the

---

7   This historical reality is analyzed in my book *Le Siècle de 1914* (Pygmalion, 2006).

USSR, the two hegemonic powers that emerged out of the Second World War. These powers then imposed their foreign models on our intellectual, social, and political traditions. Although one of the two powers has disappeared in the meantime, the poisonous effects are still felt, plunging us further into endless, unprecedented guilt. Following the eloquent words of Élie Barnavi, "the Shoah has risen to the rank of civil religion in the West."[8]

But history is never immobile. Those who have reached the summit of power are condemned to descend again.

Power, moreover, is not everything. It is necessary in order to exist in the world, to be free in one's destiny, to avoid submission to political, economic, mafia, or ideological imperialisms. But it cannot escape the diseases of the soul that have the power to destroy nations and empires.

Even before the threats posed by various very real dangers and by the oppositions of interests and intentions that are only intensifying, the Europeans of our time are, first and foremost, victims of these diseases of the soul. Indeed, this is the decisive cause of their weakness. According to those who speak in their name, they are without past, without roots, without destiny. They are nothing. And yet, what they have in common is unique. They have the privilege of the memory and models of a great civilization attested since Homer and his founding poems. But they don't know it. They have not taken stock of the novelty of the threats imposed by the era.

Iron Belt and Home Territory

In 2007, to close the year of Vauban, the tricentenary of the death of the great strategist, a magnificent work described and showed through striking aerial views the fortified places created or developed by the

---

8   Response by Élie Barnavi to Régis Debray, *À un ami israélien* (Flammarion, 2010).

indefatigable builder that was Marshal Vauban.[9] We know that we owe to him the expression "*pré carré*" [home territory] to designate the kingdom of France — a kingdom that he protected against all external threat by the "iron belt" of his fortifications.

Today, we can still contemplate a large part of these works of art, these fortifications, admirable in beauty, that were built in line with the natural escarpments. But what remains of the "iron belt" that defended our borders? Nothing. It is for this reason that new dangers mock borders. These borders are porous to the least desired migrations and to the sophisms that justify them. A head of state was able to say that he rejoiced that France is henceforth supposedly multicolored in imitation of Brazil. On this question, which engages their future and that of their descendants, the French, no more than other Europeans, have not been consulted, and they will not be. Such is the reality of democracy that only offers choice between trifles.

Before being porous to migrants, borders were porous to the invasion of ideas. They are what favored the acceptance of the unacceptable. During a debate organized on the theme "Jews and Christians," Alain Finkielkraut, with his usual lucidity, summarized the fate of Europeans with this lapidary formula: "We are nothing!"[10] Indeed, to the horrors of the 20th century, he said, "our democracies responded with the religion of humanity, that is to say with the universalization of the idea of the similar and the condemnation of everything that divides or separates men [...] This meant that, in order to no longer exclude anyone, Europe had to undo itself, 'de-originate' itself, keep from its heritage only the universalism of human rights. Such is [...] the secret of Europe. We are nothing."

Not all Europeans resign themselves to being nothing. Some are even coming around to posing the eternal question imposed by the danger: what is to be done?

---

9   Franck Lechenet and Frédéric Sartiaux, *Plein ciel sur Vauban* (éditions Cadré Plein Ciel, 2007).

10   *Le Monde* (November 11–12, 2007).

Parodying a famous formula, "Politics first," as obsolete now as Vauban's "iron belt," I will say for my part: "Mystique first." Political action is inconceivable without the prerequisite of a mystique capable of directing it and responding to the "we are nothing."

What mystique? That of the clan, of course, of sources and origins — in other words, of our tradition and our identity. One can refer on this point to Heidegger's words in his famous interview with *Der Spiegel* in 1966: "According to our experience and our human history, I know that everything essential and great could be born only from the fact that man had a homeland and was rooted in a tradition." Let it be noted that, unlike his colleagues in abstractions, the philosopher invoked "our experience and our history."

Tradition is not a composite addition. Tradition is the source of founding energies. It is the origin. And origin precedes beginning. So it is for all peoples, large or small, who have endured in their being through time: Arabs, Basques, Hebrews, Japanese, Africans, Chinese… And this is true for Europeans, rich in their small homelands and heritages that are manifold manifestations of their great tradition of princeps, those sung of long ago by the primordial poems of ancient Greece.

Being a Rebel Today

Most of my work as a meditative historian has been guided by two strong perceptions, that of the European catastrophes of the 20th century, and that of the ablation of our memory, or in other words, the consciousness of our inability to meet challenges. But now, in the evening of my life, I observe the first signs of an awakening in which I have always believed without ever hoping to see it in my lifetime.

I have never admitted that European decadence and decline were fatalities. Unlike so many intellectuals I see chattering, I was in my youth first a combatant before becoming an historian and essayist. This undoubtedly explains, provided some additional traits of temperament, a view such as mine, which is by no means conventional, of history in the making. History is not an exact science. No matter what claims one might make about it, it is not a science at all, but it uses scientific methods. It is knowledge and poetry. This knowledge is not destined for the satisfaction of researchers, professors, or scholars. Its function is to elucidate the mysteries of the past, the birth and decline of powers, the behavior and reasons of actors small and great, causes and consequences. Its function is to enlighten us about ourselves and about the uncertain world in which we live. This knowledge can restore our broken memory. It proceeds by analogies and comparisons. It is not neutral. It is a creator of meaning. This is why this knowledge is both dangerous and intoxicating for those who, beyond curiosity and distraction, draw from it their reasons to be, to act and to hope.

Thus have I seized from the past all that it could bring me so as to understand the present and smell the promises of the future, even when dark. While benefitting from one or another among them, I have stayed away from the school quarrels that have torn apart academics. Relying on knowledge of the long past of great civilizations, I do not believe in historical fatalities. Not in those imagined by Vico or Spengler any more than those theorized by Marx or, more recently, some Fukuyama. I have often explained this.

How can one not be a rebel today? On the eve of the wars of religion, in his *Discourse on Voluntary Servitude*, Étienne de La Boétie, a friend of Montaigne, pointed out the sly forms of veiled tyrannies which one suffers by closing one's eyes. In our European countries, our era is saturated with masked tyrannies. Against them, I have rebelled.

To exist is to fight what denies me. Being a rebel does not consist of collecting impious books and dreaming of phantasmagoric plots or guerrillas in the Carpathians. It means being one's own norm through fidelity to a superior norm. To hold to oneself in the face of nothingness. To be watchful so as to never 'recover' from one's youth. To prefer to put the world against oneself rather than to grovel before it. To never, in the face of setbacks, pose the question of the futility of struggle. One acts because it would be unworthy to give up, and it is better to perish fighting than to surrender.

The first act by which one refuses to be submissive always consists of freeing oneself from fear or fascination with words. Words arouse images, tonic or toxic, troubling or intoxicating. It is through words, through their seductive, perfidious, or intimidating power, that a dominant system encloses those it wants to neutralize, well before resorting to other, more formidable weapons. To choose the name by which one designates an adversary, to name him, is already to impose oneself on him, to make him enter unknowingly into one's own game, to prepare his annihilation or, conversely, to free oneself from his grip. Thus did Emperor Julian, Machiavelli, Voltaire, Nietzsche, and Solzhenitsyn, in order to be free.

Words are weapons. To give oneself one's own words, and to first give oneself a name, is to affirm one's existence, one's autonomy, one's freedom. Thus can we assume the name of rebel.

The rebel is in intimate relationship with legitimacy. He defines himself against what he perceives as illegitimate. Faced with imposture or sacrilege, he is to himself his own law by fidelity to trampled legitimacy. Rebellion first stems from the spirit before resorting to arms. The will to engage in struggle, even if hopeless, was incarnated in Sophocles' Antigone. Her example inducts us into the space of sacred legitimacy. Antigone is a rebel by fidelity. She braves Creon's decree out of respect for the tradition transgressed by the king. It matters little that Creon has his reasons. These do not cancel the sacrilege. Antigone therefore believes herself legitimized in her rebellion and accepts its price. We can take this example transmitted by Sophocles as our own. It belongs to our tradition.

The Revolt of Mothers

Rebellion is the daughter of indignation. It moves silently in drowsy consciences. And suddenly, in unforeseen fashion, it awakens where no one expected it. Thus it was for the great movement that seized a large fraction of French opinion during 2013 against the Taubira law[11] on homosexual marriage.

Originally, everyone thought this law project was one of those red herrings with which politicians amuse the gallery. And then we understood that behind the red herring had slipped one of those perverse projects by which the fanatics of deconstruction want to destroy the last foundations still structuring European societies.

The question posed by the law in no way concerned respect for the sentimental or sexual particularities of a minority. Homosexuality is not a historical novelty. It would be easy to count the illustrious personages, kings, queens or great lords of past times who preferred intimate frequentation of the same sex, and whom ancient chronicles sometimes mocked.

Private life is everyone's own affair. As long as personal preferences do not degenerate into outrageous, provocative manifestations, there

11 Ms. Taubira is originally from Cayenne (Guyana). Elected as an independentist and then socialist from Guyana, she became known by giving her name to a law voted in on May 10, 2001, which recognized the transatlantic slave trade and the slavery that resulted from it as a crime against humanity. Several historians have criticized the very principle of this law, emphasizing that the text limits the "crime" to the European trade alone, whereas the quasi-totality of African slaves had been captured not by Whites, but by African slave traders. Moreover, the trade in slaves was routine on the black continent before the arrival of Europeans. It was notably practiced by Arab slave traders. After being nominated Minister of Justice and Keeper of the Seals on May 16, 2012, following the victory of socialist candidate François Hollande in the presidential election, Ms. Taubira presented at the beginning of 2013 a law project authorizing marriage for homosexual couples, which opened the way to a sort of "right to children" for these couples and, subsequently, to the possibility of acquiring (buying) children by means of medically assisted procreation (MAP) with the assistance of "surrogate mothers" remunerated for this purpose.

is nothing to object to. In France, through the "civil solidarity pact" (PACS), the law has established a legal framework allowing two people of the same sex (or different sexes) to live together while benefiting from a series of social or fiscal advantages. This is a legal consecration of the desire for love or affection.

Marriage is something else. It does not relate to love, even if it is sometimes its consequence. Marriage is the union of a man and a woman with a view to procreation. If one removes the difference of sex and procreation, nothing remains except love, which can evaporate. Unlike PACS, marriage is an institution created with a view to children to come, not a simple contract.

This is why the gay marriage project felt like an unbearable attack on one of the ultimate foundations of our civilization. Hence the immense popular demonstrations of January 13 and March 24 that announced others. The hundreds of thousands of demonstrators (1,400,000 according to organizers) on March 24, confined to the Avenue de la Grande Armée, perceived a symbol in the name of this famous avenue. They saw themselves as the vanguard of the "great army" of those indignant at the "Taubira law."

One can destroy a civilization with the stroke of a pen. The French know this from having experienced it several times in their history since 1789 and even before. They also know from experience that it takes centuries of effort to rebuild a civilization.

After the first demonstration, the one on March 24 brought together even more participants. It even ended up occupying part of the Champs-Élysées, despite the barriers of riot police and their tear gas.

One must be blind not to see the reality of this mobilization: a mass revolt against the destruction of the family. Every child has the right to know where he comes from, who his father is and who his mother is. It is of no use to recall that, some 33 centuries ago, the Trojan War was provoked to enforce respect for the union of the Achaean king Menelaus and his wife Helen, abducted by a Trojan prince. All the kings of the Achaean federation had sworn to protect the marriage of

Helen and Menelaus. So they united to bring Helen back to her home and to her daughter Hermione. Their war had as its conclusion the destruction of Troy. This was also the pretext for the *Iliad*, the founding poem of our civilization.

The demonstration of January 13 took place in a rather playful atmosphere. The privileged who govern us treated the appeal that this peaceful crowd addressed to them with Soviet contempt. This is why the following demonstration, again bringing together entire families and a very large number of young people, including resolute boys and girls, was more tense. Once again, the people who govern us treated this popular indignation, which they could neither foresee nor understand, so poorly and with such contempt.

In doing so, they committed a grave fault. When indignation mobilizes such masses, young mothers and their children, it is a sign that a sacred part of what constitutes a nation has been transgressed beyond what is bearable. It is dangerous to provoke a revolt of mothers.

The Content of this Breviary

The meditative historian that I am felt very early on the necessity of transposing into writing his research and reflections on what he saw of his time, and what he felt as decline or awakening. The Breviary that I put forth here develops this in a new form. According to Rabelais' maxim, it seizes the "substantive marrow." This is the meaning I give to the word "breviary," a collection of writings, reflections, and examples to which one can refer each day to nourish one's thought, acts, and life.

After this prologue, the first chapter will tell the reader where I come from, what it means to be a "samurai of the West," how I was shaped by the horizon of war as well as built up by historical reflection, the source of memory and the only true antidote to the wanderings of thought.

The following chapter pertains to what I call the "metaphysics of the unlimited," in which I see the matrix of present and future catastrophes.

This "metaphysics" comes from afar. It permeates mentalities and fundamental "representations." Everything else flows from it: the domination of technology, the spirit of predatory neo-capitalism, unlimited growth, as well as the endangering of nature. Among its consequences, one can count repeated financial crises and foreseeable conflagrations in the future. One cannot think of eventual remedies if one has not identified the causes of the evil, as I propose to do.

For the sake of mental hygiene, I then propose a "detour through Japan." This highly "modern" yet traditional and refined world is an example of complete otherness in regard to Europe. And yet, we often feel an admiring empathy for the Japan of the samurai. By proposing this "detour" through another world, I suggest another look at our own. To think in a new way, we first need to escape routines.

The fourth chapter is devoted to the ablation of European memory and its reconquest through the "revolution" of tradition. This has nothing to do with those various traditions in the common sense of the word. Nor it is about any backwards-looking view. Tradition is not the past, it is what does not pass. Behind the composite appearances of our tradition, first the Greco-Roman, the Celtic as well, then the Christian, and finally the secular, one will discover the hidden perenniality of our founding tradition, the ultimate recourse for facing the troubles of spirits and comportments.

The fifth chapter proposes a return to the spiritual sources of European civilization through a renewed reading of our founding poems. The goal is to extract the ever-current meaning. Far from a scholastic or university reading of Homer, the one I undertake aims to rediscover a hidden wisdom and living principles: nature as foundation, excellence as goal, beauty as horizon.

Before the epilogue, the final chapter proposes a reflection on what the forgotten wisdom of Stoicism can bring to future Europeans, women and men, children and adults: "What depends on us." The Stoic school of behavior remained present within European Christianity, of which it was a constitutive part. But we are less interested in ancient Stoicism than in "neo-Stoicism" as a guide for life, education, and comportment for freeing oneself from perverse and provisionally triumphant deconstructions.

In the appendix, I suggest advice "for existing and transmitting."

As one will undoubtedly have understood, it is not political solutions that are outlined here, but another vision of the world and of life, drawing from our most authentic sources. It constitutes the foundation on which to build the personal life of each individual, of families, nations, and living communities. But one can also draw therefrom the principles without which any great politics is inconceivable.

CHAPTER I

A SAMURAI OF THE WEST

T HIS BREVIARY is the result of my personal reflections, the reflections of a samurai of the West who only grants himself the right to judge on the condition of paying the price for it. This Breviary draws from numerous works of scholarship which will be noted, but I alone assume responsibility for the interpretations. Before going any further, I owe it to the reader to tell him where I come from and why I have these questions and answers.

I am a writer and historian. A writer by taste and passion. Writing has long been my preferred form of expression, the one that favors my analysis, precision of thought and its nuances, the use of the exact word. It is a rather intoxicating requirement to conceive, compose, and correct one's own texts, often to escape the limits of linear writing for the spiral construction of what must become a fresco. This requirement is exercised towards oneself and towards unknown readers, unpredictable recipients of bottles loaded with meaning and entrusted to the chances of the sea. It is an exciting, exhausting, wonderful and endless asceticism. Applied to history, its aim is the hope of offering readers the pleasure of understanding the most opaque and controversial subjects, which one elucidates without simplifying them, and from which one draws new thoughts.

Learning History by Participating Therein

I have many friends who are university historians and scholars in their own field.[1]

But, for my part, I chose another path, external to teaching.

I wished to have the complete freedom to devote myself to subjects that awakened my passion for understanding beyond the beaten paths, without being subject to the administrative contingencies of the university. Yes, I have always worked with passion. A passion sharpened by the choice of extreme situations that reveal the truth of the actors, their errors, and their reasons. Sharpened also by the difficulty of controversial periods.[2] Like others before me, I came to history by way of investigations conducted according to the rules of historical research while always questioning the unknown origins of characters, phenomena, and events.

How does one become the meditative historian that I am, a creator of meaning, awakener of dreams? I do not know the recipe — so much

---

1   The occasion being thus offered to me, as far as ancient history is concerned, I wish to express my gratitude to François Chamoux, a Hellenist and Latinist, historian of the Greek and Hellenistic world. I also associate this testimony with Pierre Hadot, the former holder of the chair of ancient philosophy at the Collège de France, as well as Jean Haudry, professor of Sanskrit at the University of Lyon-III, a specialist in Indo-European languages and civilizations. All three lavished their advice and encouragement concerning my essay *Histoire et tradition des Européens* (Le Rocher, 2002; 2004), notably on the subject of my interpretation of the Homeric poems. My gratitude is also great for Lucien Jerphagnon, member of the Academy of Athens, Jean-Louis Voisin, professor of Roman history at the University of Burgundy, as well as Yann Le Bohec, professor of Roman history at the Sorbonne-Paris-IV. The great interviews that I have collected in more than 60 issues of *La Nouvelle Revue d'Histoire* also attest to my debt toward many other great historians.

2   As examples: *Histoire critique de la Résistance* (Pygmalion, 1995; 2002); *Histoire et dictionnaires de la Collaboration* (Pygmalion, 2000; 2002); *Les Blancs et les rouges. Histoire de la guerre civile russe, 1917–1921* (Pygmalion, 1997; Le Rocher, 2007); *De Gaulle, la grandeur et le néant* (Le Rocher, 2004); *L'Imprévu dans l'Histoire* (éditions Pierre-Guillaume de Roux, 2012), etc.

do the mysteries of personality and life intervene. On the other hand, I can trace succinctly the itinerary that, in my case, led to this result.

The history that has occupied me so much over the course of my life is not a cold matter. It is also not a disembodied matter. It has always been gorged with dramas, conflicts, blood, darkness, valor and beauty. It has been said that it is the trace left by men on destiny. Extended to knowledge of art, beliefs, rites, customs, transgressions, and intimate behaviors, it offers the most eloquent mirror of the permanences and ruptures which let us understand the birth, the apogee, and the death of ambitions and powers.

I discovered the intoxication and the snares that history offers by participating in it at a very young age, at a modest rank, but with total engagement. This began at the start of the distant Algerian War, which I lived on the ground, in uniform, voluntarily, at less than 20 years old. This little irregular war was for me a foundational experience. The continuation of events made me an avid witness of the *coup de force* of May 13, 1958 which allowed General de Gaulle to return to power. A supremely Machiavellian return, accompanied by a cold mystification. This provoked the revolt of the victims and the pure, with whom I identified in my own way.[3] I felt solidarity with the lost soldiers and the cruelly abandoned French of Algeria. But the utopia of multi-ethnic integration remained foreign to me. I'll add that I did not want to let the opportunity to participate in such an adventure, which rarely offers itself to a generation, escape. Everything was moving in a violent and unexpected way. Everything seemed possible. I wanted to be part of it.

We know the immediate sequel to this history, the cruel, unworthy, botched conclusion of the Algerian War. However, General de Gaulle's return to power also had positive effects on the tightening of Franco-German ties, momentary emancipation from American subjection in

---

3   I described this formative experience in *Le Cœur rebelle* (Les Belles Lettres, 1994) [republished by éditions Pierre-Guillaume de Roux, 2014].

diplomatic matters, as well as the formation of a haughty and provisionally restored image of politics.

Paradoxically, the Gaullist epoch was to conclude 10 years later,
in May '68, with a change of society and paradigms, the shift from
"grandeur" to farce, the triumph of the money-king which led to that
of "*chienlit*."[4] While awaiting a provisional turnaround of opinion, the
days of May '68 were punctuated by a rather pitiful flight to Baden-
Baden, a sort of successful "Varennes," while the State, just the day
before still full of arrogance, evaporated. These years were, above all,
the signal that marked the entry of France and Europe into the new era
of market neo-capitalism coming from the United States, the transformation of men into commodities and consuming machines. This was
done with the active support of a hegemonic intelligentsia committed
to the logic of perpetual change. These were truly fascinating years,
full of the unexpected for a young man who observed them with an
already historical gaze!

The Horizon of War and Virility

For Western Europe, devastated by the Century of 1914 and the end
of heroic dreams, May '68 constituted a border-frontier between two
worlds, the before and after.[5]

An historical analysis of behaviors would, however, broaden
the field of observation. It would take into account the inversion of
values that Europe suffered upon emerging from the two world wars
(1914–1918 and 1939–1945). In France, the effects were a bit slower. This
country remained as if in reprieve until the end of the Algerian War.

---

4   On these events, one can refer to my essay *De Gaulle, la grandeur et le néant*, op.
     cit.

5   Speaking of May '68 is a figure of speech. Germany, Italy, and the other coun-
     tries of Western Europe lived through this period of rupture in different ways,
     but with the same consequences. As for the nations of Eastern Europe, subject
     at the time to Soviet domination, it was after the intoxications of the 1990s that
     they were subjected to the law of the new merchant system.

The significance of this little war then appears quite different from those usually accorded to it: the desirable culmination of decolonization for some, the devastating death of a fragment of their homeland for others.

In reality, the salient fact eluded by historiography could be summarized differently: the end of the Algerian War made France exit history. History that had forged it spiritually as a nation and had granted it a destiny, however equivocal it might have been. Upon the conclusion of this little war, which the French felt to be the end of all wars for them, the country was delivered to the sole perspectives of the market economy, the reign of money, and mass leisure and consumption as the sole destiny.

An old country of military tradition was propelled into a mental world deprived of the horizon of conflict. A horizon that had always been its own, just as it had been that of Europe since the most distant Antiquity. No one has reflected on this mutation to any depth.[6]

My iconoclastic thesis can be formulated in a few words: the erasure of war from the horizon of our history has led to the disappearance of masculinity in Western European societies. I will explain myself.

Man (*vir* for the Romans) is only legitimized in his virility by his protective and nurturing function. Similarly, woman is legitimized in her femininity above all by the gentleness and beauty that she dispenses around her and by the perpetuation of life that she allows. To make myself understood, I will aggravate my case and force an exaggeration.

In terms of archetypes, nothing has changed since the first clan societies of hunters. The masculine archetype is always Mr. Cro-Magnon, whose wife and children expect him to bring back a deer for dinner and to protect the hearth against pillagers. As for the feminine archetype, it is always represented by Mrs. Cro-Magnon, who likes to

---

6   I devoted an article to this subject (the horizon of war) in *La Nouvelle Revue d'Histoire* no. 37 (July–August 2008).

chat with her friends of the clan, makes herself beautiful to welcome her man, gives him beautiful children, and keeps the fire of the hearth alive.

When I speak thus of the masculine as opposed to the feminine, I am not thinking of particular persons among whom all the exceptions figure. And I know well that women, in the manner of so many illustrious sovereigns, artists, educators, animators of social life, have always realized themselves well beyond the *domus*. But, as an American psychologist who had not lost his mind once wrote in a pleasant manner, men and women come from different planets. Men come from Mars and women from Venus. In other words, there exist psychically sexed aspirations, like the predominance accorded to affective life and security in women, or, inversely, to the taste for struggle and power in men.

In cinema, the world of archetypes, masculinity is incarnated by taciturn and rough actors who are at ease in conflict. They are silent and firm. On occasion, they are rather rude and unindulgent fathers. Femininity is always incarnated in cinema by touching and pretty actresses whose world is that of sensitivity and gentleness. They flee conflict. They are full of compassion towards the victims of life, sometimes even the least defensible. They are reluctant to punish, something which real women know perfectly well how to do if necessary.

As archetypes, the masculine and the feminine are the two counterparts and indispensable poles of life. They are indispensable because they are complementary. If one of the poles disappears, everything goes awry. The masculine alone would engender a world of brutality and death. The feminine alone — that's our world: fathers have disappeared, children have become capricious, soft, tyrannical little monsters. Criminals are not guilty parties, but victims or sick people who must be coddled. Psychologists multiply while monstrous psychopaths mock their victims and sneer at the judges.

Feminism against Femininity

I will persevere on this perilous terrain by saying a word about feminism, one which may be judged by its fruits. In Europe, where femininity was always respected and celebrated, feminism has added nothing to respect, perhaps it has even led to regression. It has, on the other hand, allowed women to have access to activities or functions that were closed to them. It has also recognized that maternity is not necessarily woman's vocation. Conversely, it has had the perverse consequence of denying the otherness between femininity and virility, between gentleness and roughness. An otherness that is, however, the source of mutual attraction and of all erotic relation. In other words, with the aim of feminine promotion, feminism has propagated a condemnation of virility and a devaluation of femininity that have triumphed with "gender theory" (gender studies) coming from the United States. This fashion claims that sexual identity is the result of social construction. Already in *The Second Sex*, Simone de Beauvoir wrote: "One is not born woman, one becomes it." She was inspired by Sartre's theory, according to which identity is reduced to the gaze that others cast upon us. It was idiotic, but new, therefore interesting and "marketable." The theorists of gender studies are extremist feminists and homosexuals who intend to justify their particularities by denying that there are women and men — and no doubt also that there are does and stags, hens and roosters… As this fraction of the population has a high purchasing power, its influence on the decision-makers of "advertising" is considerable. All the more so as their fads relayed by the media favor novelties and fashions on which the merchant system feeds. It is evident that for these gilded crackpots, the family model founded on the heterogeneity of the sexes and on children is also only a "social conditioning" that must be eliminated. Hence the laws or projects legalizing homosexual marriage and the adoption of children, future victims of these new "parents."

In May 2007, in *La Nouvelle Revue d'Histoire* no. 30 (dossier "Women and Power," p. 40), I published a collection of lucubrations by Madame Françoise Héritier, honorary professor at the Collège de France, for whom the physical differences between men and women come from the domination exercised by males over females during the millennia of the Paleolithic. The gentlemen apparently reserved meat for themselves, while they compelled the ladies to be vegetarians... like Hitler was. There are no limits to ideological delusions.

Exiting War and Exiting History

It is here that we find the erasure of the horizon of war among Europeans, added to the guilt born out of the earthquake of the Century of 1914 and globalized neo-capitalism. Feminism has nothing to do with it. The latter is a consequence of it and has only amplified the effects.

Speaking, as is sometimes done, of a "feminization" of our societies seems improper to me. What is at issue is their "devirilization." The signs of this are visible: the decay of education, the refusal of responsibility for crimes and misdemeanors, victimization of the guilty, psychological accompaniment to face ordeals, purely compassionate interpretations of conflicts, fear of the dangers of history, feminization of the essentially masculine functions of government, justice, and protection.

I return to the distant Algerian War. A war that was ultimately not quite murderous for the French army, but which was heartbreaking for the French people who where chased out of their homes and appalling for the 60,000 *harkis* disarmed before being delivered to the knives of the killers against whom they had engaged.

In 1962, the ignominious end of this "little" war gave the French the illusion of forever exiting from the horizon of conflicts that had founded their civilization. In the 20th century, the consequence of uncontrollable "progress," war, had toppled into the industrialization of death, which, however, did not cancel the tragic grandeur of the soldier. For the most lucid among Europeans, this cruel reality did not suppress the feeling that struggle is in any case inherent to life, the fruit of determinations and chances that elude the will, and which one must confront with a firm heart.

In France, the exit from the Algerian War rapidly evacuated what remained of the masculine part and virile values in a society already sick like all the other nations of "Western" Europe.

The Benefits of the Desert of the Tartars

One must, however, still stop for an instant on this parenthesis of the Algerian War, with its regiments of muscled paras and shaved necks, trained for some time against the slackening of the epoch. A leftist journalist, fallen for a time under the seduction of the red beret, Gilles Perrault, left an exact testimony of it. In a book entitled *The Paratroopers* (Le Seuil, 1961), he establishes a link with fascism, which also had ties with heroism and death. Perrault cites the "Prayer of the paras" accompanied by this commentary: "All the youth recites it without even knowing it. There is no question of the standard of living. The supreme skill of the paratrooper colonels is to demand everything while offering in exchange only suffering and death. No youth will ever be able to resist the attraction of this bargain, ever." It was not the ability of the colonels who often paid the high price, but a fact of nature and culture.

Perrault also cites a fragment written by Colonel Bigeard in the time of his splendor: "We had appointments, at each corner of the trail, behind each peak, but it was with our death. That, no beast in the world could have understood." The comments of a journalist: "Fascists and paras refuse the suffering of the Christian religion because it represents submission to a divine will. The Christian accepts suffering; Bigeard seeks it. He goes to it proudly, not with humility. Accepted suffering brings the Christian closer to his God; sought suffering makes the fascist a god."

At the risk of aggravating my case, relying on all that I have learned from history, I know that the presence, even veiled, of war is what gives meaning and poetry to a society, allows it to constitute itself and maintain itself, not to be a shapeless crowd, but a people, a city, a nation. This horizon of war, confined to the *limes*, allowed Rome to hold for centuries, despite its mad emperors and its debauched crowds.[7]

Such is the paradox of war! It is at the heart of two famous novels of the 20th century, *The Desert of the Tartars* by Dino Buzzati and *The Shore of the Syrtes* by Julien Gracq. Both describe old societies in decline which yet remain standing more or less upright, not by the reality of war, but by the very thought of it that is upheld on the frontiers.

The Algerian War was a little war at our frontiers. It delayed our fall for some time. Algeria was our "desert of the Tartars."

This is how I, a young soldier in that era, without knowing anything of what I know now, perceived it intuitively.

My Initiation Began Very Early

This distance of gaze was not always my lot. For more than 10 years, before retiring definitively from the game, I was a precocious and very involved actor. My militant activism was punctuated by imprisonments. Among others were 18 months spent behind bars, from April

---

7   The history of the United States does not contradict these observations. Even before 1776, the English colonies of America had always lived in the horizon of war, facing the Indians or the French. This spur made for a good match with the spirit of capitalism (Max Weber), as with the egalitarian system well observed by Tocqueville. Unlike Europe, victim of the traumas of 1914–1918 and 1939–1945, the United States continued to live in the horizon of war, of which American cinema bears witness among others, so inclined as it is to pugnacity in comparison with European cinema. This permanence has long limited the destructive effects of neo-capitalism, of which the United States is, however, the inventor. But it is well known that an organism accustomed to a disease resists it better than recently contaminated victims.

1961 to October 1962. Such were the sanctions for the project of an armed assault on the Élysée Palace which would have logically resulted in some deaths, including my own. Political prison is a place of observation, full of teachings on human behavior in agitated periods, its possible grandeurs and its miseries. Chance had willed that I be detained in the special division of La Santé prison, which grouped the 30 or so most important civilian and especially military figures, generals and colonels of the insurrectional movement of the time. Thanks to this, by observing them daily while external events made them react intensely, I no doubt learned about the springs of history and its actors, great or small, more than I ever could have at university.

My initiation had in fact begun much earlier, in the last years of the Second World War and the Occupation, between my seventh and ninth year. What certain children see counts more in the secret alchemy of their formation than adults imagine. Allied bombings on Paris with very exciting flights toward the shelters, the unforgettable presence of German uniforms, radio communiqués, the battles of the Liberation, deaths seen very close, blood on the sidewalks, spectacular reversals of opinion noted from one hour to the next in my close environment, under my mute gaze as a terribly attentive child. And above all, a general atmosphere that was unrelated to what I saw described later in amnesiac or fabricated accounts.

The experience of the troubled years of the Algerian War, after the memories of summer 1944, was well worth that of the wars of religion or the Fronde. To have lived through a tumultuous era up close is an immense asset for the meditative historian. I thus discovered that the courage of a radical opponent in a period of civil war requires a nerve that makes that of the heroes of regular war pale. The latter receive their legitimacy and the satisfactions of glory from society. Conversely, the radical opponent must draw his justifications from himself, confront general reprobation, the aversion of the great number, and a repression without brilliance. Machiavelli knew this. He would not have become what he was without the experience of his own setbacks and the troubles of Florence.

After having learned about history by participating in it, I learned to write by writing it.

Constant meditation on the subjects I have studied has left traces which I shall summarize.

A Response to the Exhaustion of Thought

I learned to study history according to the method of source criticism. I learned to lay bare the springs of behaviors and not to stick to the conventions of reassuring opinions. I also learned to compose the tableau of an epoch, the narrative of an event, the portrait of actors, by devoting myself with passion to what belongs more to art than to science. One does not describe a civil war like the loves of Paul and Virginia.

Several of my books, however documented, nourished, and structured they may be, are essays. An essay is a work in which the author proposes an interpretation while respecting the rules of intellectual honesty (concealing nothing that would contradict his opinion), and without yielding to anachronism (judging a bygone epoch according to today's criteria). Historical study lends itself particularly to the essay. Its field of reflection is unlimited. Freeing itself from the abstractions and artifices of philosophical or sociological concepts, it sees true men, not Plato's "Ideas" or the reductive convention of social categories. It apprehends the real in all its complexity, offering endless responses to the exhaustion of contemporary thought.

History is the domain of the unexpected. No one in the world around 1900 could have imagined what would be the extraordinary unfolding of the 20th century and its reversals, the major catastrophe of the two world wars, the disappearance of empires and great monarchies (except in Great Britain), the decline of old Europe, and, later, decolonization, the emergence or renaissance of new powers in Asia and elsewhere, the appearance of new forms of society. This is how it has always been, but rarely in proportions so sudden, gigantic, and universal.

Nothing is ever truly predictable in history, which philosophers who reason by categories and not in the concrete do not always know. The great historical unknown resides in men, their "representations," their ambitions, their blindness, their revolts, their aptitudes, and the mystery of their destiny. Without Lenin and Trotsky in Petrograd in 1917, no Bolshevik Revolution. Without Hitler in Berlin in 1933, no Third Reich. Without Churchill in London in 1940, not the same war, with all that followed for Europe and the world. Beyond geography, only one component keeps its stability through time: civilizations and their own tradition, even when this can sometimes seem eclipsed. This is why the stakes of history are always the space and the soul of peoples, in the atavistic sense of the word.

I must stop for an instant on the specific approach that mine is. It weaves the fabric of this Breviary as well as a whole portion of my writings. In effect, it is what connects historical reflection and the quest for spirituality.

Faced with the failures of religions and philosophical systems to respond to the question of the meaning of life for our epoch, I draw responses from history. It is through history and awakened memory that I rediscover the forgotten foundations of European spirituality.[8]

---

8   Having developed my reflections on history and memory in *Histoire et tradition des Européens* (2002; 2004) as well as in *Le Choc de l'Histoire* (2011) [*The Shock of History: Religion, Memory, Identity*, trans. Charlie Wilson (London: Arktos, 2015)], I will not take them up again here. However, one can refer to the new developments of chapter 4 of this Breviary, "Forgotten Memory."

CHAPTER II

THE METAPHYSICS OF THE UNLIMITED

W E HAVE health and comfort like never before, and knowledge, understanding, and freedoms without equal. And yet,
there lurks in Europe the feeling of a veiled decline, a sort of flabby
nihilism perceptible in what passes for literature or official art. Beauty
has deserted our lives to shut itself away in museums. Our most
beautiful streets are drowned in a swarming of haggard and motley
crowds. Why has ugliness replaced beauty? Why this desert of culture
and identity in the midst of colossal and very unequal prosperity?
Why has money become the only standard, crushing us under its
vulgarity and masked power?

The Century of Excess

To attempt an answer, first a general observation about the 20th century, of which our era is an extension. This century was one of excess
in proportions hitherto unknown. Political and military excess during
the two world wars, large-scale destruction, mass massacres, terror
bombings, recourse to terrorism and, to crown the horror, two atomic
bombs dropped on civilian populations. The excess of technology
amplified in truly unimaginable ways the means of production, rapid

transport, destruction, and death. In *Man and Technics*,[1] published in 1931, Oswald Spengler already described the "diabolical" character of human dominion over nature. "Faustian thought," he wrote, "begins to feel nauseous with machines."

During the two world wars, we saw in all things the effects of extreme excess, the hubris[2] that the Ancients condemned. We observed them subsequently in giant and uncontrollable financial speculations, in the sudden weakening of the largest companies, in major ecological disasters and in the endangering of a planet subjected to the excesses of profit, technical predation, and unlimited growth, which prodigious medical advances or immense creations of goods cannot compensate for. This excess has historically identifiable causes. But one would be mistaken to limit oneself only to simple productivist chains. The role of "representations" is essential.

Modern and technologically developed societies are not only dependent on financial powers. They are prisoners of their economic growth, which is the condition of their existence and of their survival in the competition of powers. Growth is a vital necessity for these societies, of which it is the engine. Without growth, losing their main justification, these societies would collapse. Now growth itself is dependent on the consumption of useless goods; in other words, on the waste of resources of each country and the planet in general. Certainly, we hear criticisms, some measures are enacted, advertising campaigns are orchestrated around "global warming" and other spectacular themes that make a lot of money for those who launch them.[3] But waste and

---

1   Oswald Spengler, *Man and Technics: A Contribution to a Philosophy of Life*, trans. Charles Francis Atkinson and Michael Putman (London: Arktos, 2015).

2   The term hubris that we find originally in Homer's poems signifies unjust violence, insolence, and outrage, passionate excess in words and acts. The Greek verb *hubritzein* means to commit excesses and to use illegitimate violence. The violence of men called for the violence of the gods through the intervention of Nemesis, goddess of divine indignation and just vengeance.

3   It is far from my intention to deny the ecological nuisances caused by the excesses of the world of technology (the Titans invoked by Jünger). One cannot,

the irresponsible predation of natural wealth nonetheless remain a vital requirement of extreme capitalism, including in its Chinese version. Thus, in the 50 years of intensive growth at the end of the 20th century, the natural heritage was liquidated — reserves in fossil fuels, forest and marine biodiversity, plant cover ensuring the renewal of oxygen, etc. — all of which had slowly formed since the origins of the Earth. And this liquidation has only accelerated since.

Growth and Progress in Question

One could, of course, dream of an immobile technological society without waste. It would produce machines, instruments, and objects made to last.

Such was the case in Europe until around 1950. It's finished, because growth and the logic of extreme profit require so. Even the houses are not built to last. Machines, computers, and other electronic devices are programmed to degrade automatically after a reduced usage time. Waste is constitutive of a system that has as its foundation a metaphysics of the unlimited. A metaphysics which, as we shall see, was slowly introduced into the European psyche by a prosaic variant of the almighty God of the Bible and which took its rise from the 16th century of our era.

One of the crucial questions of the future will be that of stopping growth, and better yet that of degrowth.[4] But is it possible to conceive of an exit from the system of unlimited growth other than through pious wishes or incantations without effects? Can one imagine the price to pay for a worldwide policy of degrowth and anti-consumerism, the condition for the survival of peoples, cultures, and nature?

Let us be lucid: never will a halt to growth result from a voluntary decision by States. It would entail such a retreat in apparently easy

---

however, ignore their exploitation for purposes that are by no means innocent.

4   Hervé Juvin, *Produire le monde. Pour une croissance écologique* (Gallimard, 2008); Alain de Benoist, *Demain, la décroissance!* (Edite, 2009).

living habits that it would inevitably provoke revolutionary troubles and the overthrow of the authority that would have prescribed it. This means that we will press forward again and again down this path to the point of great financial, ecological, and political catastrophes, which everything suggests are imminent without our being able to imagine what forms they will take. However, changes in representations are perceptible in the opinion of European and Western countries.

"Better" Opposes "More"

The public discovers that sciences and technologies have a price and are not uniquely beneficial. Optimism regarding the future has crumbled. The motive for infinite hope at the beginning of the 20th century, scientific knowledge, and "progress" are viewed a century later with a certain mistrust. The anxiety caused by worldwide demographic growth and the aging of populations in the Northern Hemisphere is augmented by the unease provoked by awareness of the danger posed by the pillaging of natural resources, massive pollution, nuclear proliferation (both civilian[5] and military), and the accelerated development of genetic manipulations and other biotechnologies.

Under the impact of these threats, we perceive a revolution of minds that is not political. A revolution of "representations" and behaviors. The idea is spreading that, in order to live better, one should perhaps consume less. In these changes, a role is played by medicine, confronted with questions of nutrition and health, quality of life at birth, and also the desire to die with dignity.

One cannot ignore the change in mentality that the ecological spirit represents, to which the market system itself is forced to adapt. At bottom, it would be about substituting for the metaphysics of the unlimited a metaphysics of limit, the idea that "better" opposes

---

5   Despite the promises of the concerned authorities, the treatment of radioactive waste has remained at a standstill. The only method used, burial, is in no way a real treatment.

"more," that one should consume less and free oneself from the madness of waste, from the consumerist drug. A change in behavior cannot be conceived without a modification of "representations." This is underway. Economic growth cannot indeed be apprehended in isolation. It is only one of the manifestations of the metaphysics of the unlimited and the universal imperialism of technology.

This is an incommensurable difference with ancient times, those sung of by Homer, Hesiod, and Ovid. Our distant ancestors respected Nature, even if they feared its dangers. They had an intimate consciousness of the unity of the world, which they felt as a harmony of conflicts. They knew themselves to be dependent on the mysterious forces that command its balances and are configured by the gods.

Nature had a soul. It was animated. It manifested in all things its universal divinity. The woods, moors, and springs were peopled with nymphs, sprites or fairies. And our ancestors respected its sacrality.

The Sacrality of Nature

Our myths and our rites sought a coincidence between human works and the image of an ordered cosmos. The circular arrangement of the solar temple of Stonehenge thus reflected the order of the world, symbolized by the course of the sun, its perpetual return at the end of night and at the end of winter. It figured the ring of life uniting birth and death. It also represented the eternal cycle of the seasons.

Likewise, the Greek temples were born from the sacred wood of the Hyperborean ancestors. Strabo says that "the poets who embellish everything name 'sacred wood' any sanctuary, even stripped of vegetation." Archaeological research has shown that the columns of archaic Greek temples were formed of tree trunks. The analogy between temple and sacred forest moves us. The roughly carved effigies of divinities were originally set up in consecrated groves. Pausanias enumerates the species that best suited the sacred groves: oaks, ash trees, plane trees, olive trees, pines, cypresses. Echoing the ancient authors, Varro specifies that the temple is "a space limited by trees." The sacred wood formed the enclosure, the peribolos of the divine domain. It gave birth to the peristyle that characterizes the Greek temple of the classical epoch. This is the stylized reminder of the original forest, habitat of the divinities of the Greek pantheon.[6] Architecture configures this place of divine space (*numen inest*, writes Ovid) where sacrality is concentrated. The external colonnade is the image of vegetation whose stems spring from the soil to form a place of convergence between men and divinities in the sunlight. At Olympia, the venerable temple of Hera, built in the 7th century before our era, allows us to follow the "petrification" of the external portico, initially built in wood, and whose shafts were progressively replaced by Doric columns in stone. Thus, a sort of stylized forest accompanied the sanctuary when it, having left wild nature, occupied the center of cities.

Despite the ruptures with the ancient European order introduced by biblical interpretations, the construction of Romanesque or Gothic churches still responded to ancient symbolisms. Built on ancient sacred sites, they ensured their perpetuation.[7]

They continued to be "oriented" in relation to the rising sun, and their sculptures were all rustling with a fantastic bestiary. In its impressive surge, the stone grove of Romanesque and Gothic naves remained the transposition of ancient sacred forests.

However, a fundamental rupture was advancing, one which would disassociate humans from nature and postulate the vain and senseless idea that the universe had been created for men alone. By defining man as "master and possessor of nature," by seeing in animals "machines," Descartes only theorized what had been prepared by the separation

---

6   See on this subject Henri Stierlin, *Grèce. De Mycènes au Parthénon* (Taschen, 2001). The author is a specialist in sacred architecture.

7   In 1711, four pillars were discovered under the choir of the Notre-Dame de Paris, called "of the boatmen," dating back to the 1st century of our era. They represent Celtic divinities once celebrated in a Gallo-Roman temple on the site where the Christian cathedral was built 12 centuries later.

from nature inherent in the monotheistic religions born in the deserts of the Orient. He expressed the logic of nihilism, anticipating the technological arrogance leading to the manipulation of the living. He announced the universe of the universal megalopolis, built in hatred of Nature.

Nature Loves to Hide

But what exactly is Nature? Is the rose in my garden Nature? Yes and no. Yes, for the reason that it could perhaps live and renew itself without my help. No, insofar as it is a "fabrication" of learned gardeners, without whom it would not be what it is. So, what is Nature? Answer: Nature is what exists and lives by its own movement, without human intervention or despite it. According to Aristotle's definition, it is what possesses in itself its principle of becoming. Wind, tides, vipers, woodcock, deer, wasps, moray eels, foxes, fallow land, and the flow of water after rain are of nature. But the rose bed, the field of transgenic wheat, and the sanitized orchard are no longer quite of nature and they will be less and less so. They are domesticated nature, on life support.

Day after day, researchers penetrate some new secrets, substituting themselves for nature so as to exploit, constrain, or change it. Yesterday, the cloning of a sheep, today the fertilization of a mouse without a male…

An historian of thought and the longtime holder of the chair of ancient philosophy at the Collège de France, Pierre Hadot opened some major paths for reflection on our relations with Nature in his book *The Veil of Isis: Essay on the Idea of Nature*.[8] He explores the opposing ideas that Europeans have formed of Nature for 3,000 years, examining the successive interpretations given to the famous aphorism of Heraclitus: "Nature loves to hide." This examination begins with Homer, two centuries before Heraclitus. It is indeed in the *Odyssey* that we find for the first time the word and concept of nature that the Greeks call *physis*

---

8   Pierre Hadot, *Le Voile d'Isis. Essai sur l'idée de Nature* (Gallimard, 2004).

(from which comes "physics"). In Homer and in Greek thought before Plato, the word *physis* designates the animating force of the cosmos and of life: the nature of a plant as well as that of an animal or that of a man. *Physis* is always the nature of something.

From Plato and Aristotle onward, the word's meaning changes. It designates less the force than its result. Nature, henceforth endowed with a capital letter, becomes somewhat synonymous with the universe (cosmos) and its organizing principle.

Thus, Heraclitus' adage will take on the now current significance: Nature carries within it "secrets" over which men are divided. Some want to pierce them with more or less curiosity and violence, others hold to respecting their mystery and making them a source of joy and wisdom. To characterize these two dispositions that have traversed the history of European thought, Pierre Hadot relied on the opposing myths of Prometheus and Orpheus. For the latter, one could substitute that of Artemis, protector of wild nature. Seeing in Nature an enemy and then disenchanted matter, Prometheus seeks to make it confess its secrets to transform them into instruments of power. He seeks to make it confess its secrets in order to dominate it, thus anticipating the biblical injunction: "Subdue nature" (Genesis 1:28). Conversely, Artemis, associated with measure and finitude, is indignant at this violence "against nature," advocating before Lucretius, Spinoza, Goethe, or Nietzsche that we merge with the immanence of Nature and respect its "modesty."

With the exception of the ancient hunting peoples, of whom we are nevertheless descendants and heirs, men are not always friends of Nature. They often distrust and fear it, even when they claim to protect it. In their professed love of Nature and animals, most Europeans are an exception compared to the rest of humanity. Elsewhere, in the Orient, in Africa, in Asia, or in America, other men often flee nature when it is true, living, wild. They fight and destroy it. It repulses and frightens them. It is sometimes the same in Europe, too, for city people.

Why Something Rather than Nothing?

Nature causes anxiety, not only through what it reveals as fearsome when one finds oneself at night alone in a forest, at sea, or in the mountains. Nature causes anxiety especially because it is inexplicable. It is refractory to understanding. It escapes the principle of reason that wants everything to have a reason for being that explains it (Leibniz). Why the world? Because... God for example. And why God? Because the world... But what proves to us that reason is right? Why would the mystery of the world let itself be pierced by the little reason of men? How and why could we understand everything, explain everything, since this "everything" precedes us, contains us and surpasses us?

What disconcerts and worries us is that Nature pursues no goal. It does not listen to us. It asks nothing of us. It does not concern itself with us. It was not created for us. But it encompasses us. It is free. Nothing external to it governs it, as storms, tsunamis or volcanic eruptions remind us from time to time. According to Lucretius' word, it is both uncreated and creative. It is without thought, without consciousness, without will.

No one has better translated the anxiety and even horror of Nature than Jean-Paul Sartre in his philosophical novel *Nausea* (1938). We know that, in a short essay published in 1946, Sartre defined his existentialism as a humanism. By humanism, he meant a form of philosophy that places man at the center of creation. The certainty that "I think, therefore I am" is a truth is for him the basis of existentialism. But a question immediately arises: "Why do I think?" At this very instant, his existentialism confronts the unjustifiable character of existence. Taking up Leibniz's interrogation, he responds: there is no reason for there to be something rather than nothing. Sartre is an anxious and disenchanted rationalist, watched by nothingness.

Roquentin, the existentialist hero of *Nausea*, remains Cartesian. But, like Sartre, he is a revolted rationalist. He discovers indeed that reason cannot account for concrete existence. The pebble that

Roquentin holds in his hand while walking along the shore gives birth to nausea in him. He may well define the properties of the pebble, its mineral composition, its color, its form and other properties, yet its existence remains totally inexplicable. Why a pebble rather than nothing?

However, for an exasperated humanist like Roquentin, a pebble is less irritating than a tree. Roquentin's nauseating crisis reaches its summit during his walk in a park, where he encounters a chestnut tree. The silence of the tree, its immutable pose, its roots in the soil, its branches in the sky, its implicit refusal to let its existence be reduced to a concept — all this offends Roquentin, fills him with disgust. Overwhelmed by examining a root of the chestnut tree, Roquentin kicks it, without managing to damage the bark.

A tree is more philosophically opaque than a pebble. Roquentin is confined within the limits of human consciousness, beyond which exists Nature, independent, autonomous, indifferent. Now, whatever escapes the world of human intelligibility, of mathematical intelligibility, terrifies him. Roquentin is therefore condemned to the city, the ultimate fortress of humanism and rationality. But Roquentin feels that one day, as in Vico's predictions, vegetation will triumph over the city. This fills him with terror.

Horror for Sartre, Joy for Giono

What is horror for Sartre is joy for Giono. The contrast between the imagination of these two writers corresponds to two opposite ways of perceiving Nature. In a novella dated 1932, the author of *Song of the World* lets himself enter a somewhat mad dream that should not be taken as an anticipation, but rather as a pantheist reverie:[9] "There will

---

9   Jean Giono, *Solitude de la pitié* (Gallimard, 1932). In the early years of the 21st century, companies of wild boars took up residence in Berlin, in the heart of the city. Similarly, litters of foxes have invaded London since the ban on fox hunting.

be happiness for you only on the day when the great trees will burst the streets, when the weight of lianas will bring down the obelisk and bend the Eiffel Tower; when, before the ticket windows of the Louvre we will hear only the light sound of ripe pods and wild seeds that fall: the day when, from the caverns of the metro, dazzled wild boars will emerge trembling from the queue…"

Following Leibniz, Sartre worries to the point of nausea at not being able to explain the why of the world. Why is there something instead of nothing? As for Giono, he looks at the world. He does not think it, he does not question it, he perceives, tastes, and admires it. He does not try to enclose it in a discourse. He walks, he contemplates. He lets himself be penetrated by this evidence, this wonder: there is something, and not nothing! This something is without "why." One thinks of the last lines of *The Stranger*, a nevertheless very nihilistic novel by Albert Camus, whose hero, on the eve of dying, experiences an unexpected sensation: "The marvelous peace of this sleeping summer entered me like a tide."

Happy are those who have lived moments of plenitude in the contemplation of Nature, what Romain Rolland called the "oceanic feeling." A gratuitous and intense sensation that the simple spectacle of clouds in a spring sky or frost on trees in winter can offer, but so can the sight of long undulations with no other limit than distant woods, a vast circus of mountains under snow, or the moving immensity of the sea. It is an intoxicating experience which alters one's state of consciousness. The experience of harmony between oneself and Nature.

The feeling of being united with the universe does not mean that one merges into an indistinct chaos. Rather, quite to the contrary, one observes the distinctions of Nature. At the beginning of the *Theogony*, Hesiod strongly shows that life without order destroys itself. Zeus and the Olympian gods came to order the cosmos to allow life. And this functions by distinction and separation.

One can follow the Hellenist Paul Mazon in his commentaries on his translation of the *Theogony* (Les Belles Lettres, 1982): "The mysterious force that gives birth to life, if nothing comes to regulate and contain it, creates only confusion and death: it immediately destroys what it has just brought to light." This is the meaning of the myth of Uranus, then of his mutilation by Kronos, and finally of Zeus' victory over the latter and over the Titans.

The Distant Origins of Murderous Progress

Exponential growth, the pillaging of nature, and its subjugation to the excessive appetites of men, all peoples combined — these are phenomena born from the idea that man as a species is at the center of the cosmos, that nature was created to satisfy his lusts and caprices. This idea, which the Ancients would have firmly rejected, took on unforeseeable proportions only very slowly, in the wake of Christian anthropocentrism. One of the most enlightening analyses of this evolution has been carried out by a Catholic theologian, Eugen Drewermann, in a book that made some noise, *Murderous Progress.*[10]

Taking care to go to the sources, the German theologian recalls that primitive Christianity was heir among others of the desert religions. "The New Testament," he writes, "was born in a very narrow cultural framework: its image of the world is not fundamentally different from that of the Old Testament; from the point of view of the natural sciences, the knowledge of the Greeks had already surpassed it centuries before it was even written, which unfortunately led to the prolongation of Judaic anthropocentrism for a period of 1,500 years despite all common sense."

---

10 Eugen Drewermann, *Le Progrès meurtrier* (Paris: Stock, 1993), p. 136. The original German edition dates from 1981. Born in 1940, Eugen Drewermann, ordained priest in 1966, is the author of a three-volume thesis on the structures of Evil (1977–1978). He taught at the Catholic University of Paderborn until 1991. He was banned by the local bishop in 1989 after the success of his essay *Fonctionnaires de Dieu* ("Functionaries of God"), which criticized certain excesses on the part of the ecclesiastical bureaucracy. This book was translated by Albin Michel in 1993.

Drewermann retraces the genesis of Judaism and, later, of Islam. Unable to expect anything from a sterile and pitiless nature, the nomads of the dry solitudes of Sinai and Arabia had fixed their hopes on the imploration of a fearsome and all-powerful divinity that emerged from the imagination of their prophets. Foreign to the cosmos, their unique God, creator of all things and tribal protector, concentrated in his person all the sacred, condemning as impious the sacrality of springs, mountains, woods, and their familiar inhabitants, that is to say, the benefits granted by Nature outside of his intervention: "There is no god but God."

When Nature Is Subject to Man

This representation was translated by a radical anthropocentrism, present in the first chapter of Genesis, when Yahweh declares: "Let us make men in our image, and let them dominate the fish of the sea, the birds of the sky, all wild beasts and those that crawl on the Earth" (Gen. 1:26). We find this injunction several times: "Be fruitful, fill the earth and subdue it" (Gen. 1:28). And again at the exit from Noah's Ark: "Be fruitful, multiply on the Earth and dominate it" (Gen. 9:1–7).

Having adopted the biblical God, albeit profoundly modifying him under Hellenistic influences, and having made him a universal divinity transplanted outside his original habitat, nascent Christianity factored in his anathemas and his prescriptions against Nature. The new religion decreed the death of the spirits of springs and woods, considered as superstitions all the more condemnable as they were in competition with the new God who affirmed himself unique. It gradually made Nature something soulless, "inanimate," which it became licit to use and abuse. With the nymphs, fairies, and sprites chased from the moors, woods, and rivers, desacralized Nature could be studied, exploited, manipulated like inert matter. The new religion placed man at the center of creation, provided that he fear God.[11]

Won over little by little to the new belief, the men of the West seemed at first to find their account in the upheaval that raised them "in the image of God," above other beings and the cosmos. Just as man was subject to God, Nature was subject to man. It is said in the Scriptures: "Subdue it" — which was taken up by various theologians, notably Thomas Aquinas in the *Summa contra Gentiles* (III, 112). The friendly agreement with Nature was finished.

As in the manner of any spiritual upheaval, the one just outlined was slow to produce effects. In the Middle Ages, the animal is still frequently represented in religious statuary, where in principle it should have had no business. Romanesque art and then Gothic art still accorded it a non-negligible place. It is often transposed into a fabulous creature by Celtic imagination. Celtic legends indeed show that the faculty of communicating with sacred animality had not been lost. Overflowing with Celtic spirituality, the literature of the Middle Ages embroiders from the 12th century on the theme of the forest, a perilous universe, but also a source of purification for the soul of the knight, whether he be named Lancelot, Perceval, Tristan, or Yvain. By capturing a stag or a boar, the noble hunter appropriates its force and spirit. In the *Lai de Tyolet*, by killing the roe deer, the hero becomes capable of understanding the spirit of wild nature which he has penetrated.[12]

The Idea of the Unlimited

Weaving the thread of the slow evolution that led from Christianity to the atheism of the Enlightenment, Eugen Drewermann showed that it was the consequence of the rupture with Nature: "Christianity,

---

11   The aphorism stated by Protagoras (cited in Plato's eponymous dialogue), "man is the measure of all things," does not mean that man is central in the universe, but that there is no reality except through the interpretation that men give of it.

12   See Gaston Paris, "*Lais inédits de Tyolet, de Guingamor, de Doom, du Lecheor et de Tydorel*," *Romania* no. 8, 1879.

which set the human being against the calming influence of nature, must confront in exchange the balance sheet of his efforts: the result is a man who, out of fear of himself and his most natural instincts, no longer has confidence either in himself or in the ambient nature [...] After showing itself to be incapable of admitting the simple natural givens that are illness, old age and death, Christianity has engendered a mentality which, following the 'death' of God, due to the despair of disappointed piety, continues to sacrifice to the former anthropo-centric morality by striving to anchor the promises of salvation on earth."[13] Thus proceeded the passage to the religion of Progress that issued forth from the scientific and economic revolution of the modern epoch. Drunk with presumption, the new "master and possessor" of Nature described by the Bible and by Descartes has done so much that, at the dawn of the 21st century, he has put it in mortal peril.

Without contemporaries understanding well the scope of these changes, another way of perceiving life and things has thus insinuated itself into minds over several centuries. In replacement of the multiple richness of the gods of European polytheism, limited in their powers, the worship of a unique God, said to be demiurge and all-powerful, introduced into minds the idea of the unlimited. Since men had been created in the image of an omnipotent and omniscient God, they themselves participated in the renunciation of limits that had been the foundation of Greek wisdom.

Athena at the Boundary Stone

Conscious of this evolution, Martin Heidegger, from the writing of *Being and Time* (1927), had defined the contemporary world in terms of the disappearance of measure and limit. He illuminated this notion of limit by describing the high relief of the Acropolis museum in Athens known as "Pensive Athena" or "Athena at the Boundary Stone": "Athena appears as she who meditates. Toward what is the meditative

---

13   E. Drewermann, op. cit., pp. 110, 136–138.

gaze of the goddess turned? Toward the boundary stone, toward the limit."[14]

The limit is not only the frontier where something stops. The limit means that by which something gathers itself, manifesting its plenitude. Europe thus found in the *Iliad* and *Odyssey* the measure of its poetic art and its literature. "It is there, at the dawn of the West, that poetry reveals its voluntary limit. It could become the voice of the Whole, but it is only the vision of the limit, nothing other than a few days of the Trojan War, or a part of Odysseus' return to Ithaca. The Whole remains inaccessible."[15]

It is indeed by its voluntary limit that the beauty of the work of art manifests itself, be it statue, fresco, edifice, poem. One thinks of Boileau's sentence: "Who cannot limit himself never knew how to write." A statement that Heraclitus, in his time, had enlarged into a philosophical axiom: "Excess [*Hubris*] must be extinguished more than fire." The adage was inscribed in the continuity of Apollonian commandments: "nothing in excess," "know thyself," "hate excess."

In absolute rupture with ancient wisdom, the reason of the Moderns, Christian or atheist, has sought to do away with the enchantment of Nature along with the perception of necessary limits and the tragic sentiment of life cultivated ever since Homer. It placed itself under the sign of the Enlightenment and their unlimited promises. Making this observation in *The Sense of Excess*, philosopher Jean-François Mattéi comments: "Man was going to deploy his humanity through the advances of science, the conquests of technology, the triumph of capitalism and the victory of democracy."[16] In his time, Nietzsche had recognized the hypocrisy that the alliance of these four figures of rationality had established: science, technology, capitalism, and democracy. They claim to incarnate the wisdom of man while

---

14 Martin Heidegger, conference at the Academy of Sciences and Arts of Athens (April 4, 1967), collected in *Les Cahiers de L'Herne* no. 45 (1983), p. 86.

15 Pietro Citati, *La Pensée chatoyante* (Gallimard, "Folio," 2004), p. 57.

16 Jean-François Mattéi, *Le Sens de la démesure* (éditions Sulliver, 2009), p. 170.

they have fanned all his excesses: "Measure is foreign to us, let us recognize it; our itch is precisely the itch of the infinite, of the immense.
Like the rider carried away by a foaming steed, we let go the reins
before the infinite, we modern men, we semi-barbarians."[17]

Prometheus Condemned

The modern universe of technology is rightly qualified as Promethean.
The allusion to the myth of Prometheus applies to the violation of the
limits and secrets of Nature. Antiquity had condemned this violation
as extreme excess, opposing it with Apollonian measure. Despite their
numerous discoveries, their mathematical knowledge and their admirable architectural science, the ancient Greeks never had the design of
enslaving Nature. They voluntarily contained themselves within the
limits of a measure that did not put nature in peril.

There exists no necessary teleological relation (*telos*: goal) leading
from the first club to the rocket. In its unlimited character, the titanic
world of technology is not the ineluctable prolongation of the first tool
(weapon) brandished by primitive men. It is its excess. For a long time,
in Europe and elsewhere, technology did not obey an internal logic
of irresistible expansion. For a long time, it was dependent on human
"representations" that limited its developments. Thus, the idea that
the Greeks formed of the Good and their sacralization of nature led
them to limit the applications of their nonetheless immense knowledge. Technology was in accord with the cosmos and did not aim to
dominate it.

Until the 16th century, China had nothing to envy in Europe in
matters of science and technology. The three great inventions that
revolutionized the world — printing, the compass, and gunpow-
der — are Chinese inventions attested since the 11th century. Yet, the
Confucian wisdom of moderation of passions that inspired their

---

17   Friedrich Nietzsche, *Par-delà bien et mal*, trans. P. Wotling (Flammarion, 2008),
      § 224, p. 655.

leaders protected them against the systematic exploitation of these inventions. Under the Ming, in the 15th century, Emperor Chenghua even ordered the destruction of the great fleets built by his predecessors. This decision turned China away from the conquest of the Indian Ocean and from high-performance naval constructions. In a utilitarian and anachronistic strategic perspective, one might think that this was an error that exposed China to the power of Westerners. But that is another matter. It does not annul reflection on the voluntary limits that it is possible to impose on technology outside a situation of competition or conflict.

The Excess of Technology

The "Promethean" shift of technology occurred in Europe only slowly, under the effect of a series of earthquakes of historical, intellectual, and spiritual order which began at the end of the 15th century. They gradually gave immense practical scope to the metaphysics of the unlimited present at the origin in Christian consciousness. If one wants to chronologically enumerate these events of giant effects, one can place at the fore the discovery of America in 1492. A prodigious event that modified all existing representations. In the order of symbols, it overturned the prohibition of *Non plus ultra* that, as is said, Hercules would have had engraved on the two columns of the Strait of Gibraltar, at the limits of the known world, forbidding humans from venturing beyond. Charles V violated the prohibition by proudly changing the ancient motto to "*Plus ultra.*"

Simultaneously, the great intellectual shocks of the Renaissance, the Reformation, and the Catholic Counter-Reformation provoked a fundamentalist rereading of the Scriptures, arousing conquering proselytisms. These contributed to engaging the future American power and Europe in the race for world domination. The metaphysics of the unlimited henceforth imposed itself in facts.

It benefited from instruments suddenly offered by the scientific revolution introduced by the empirico-mathematical method owed to Galileo, Kepler, Descartes, Newton, and their successors. Later, the worldwide expansion of Europe, the prospects of profit and universal competition between powers granted unlimited deployment to the pretensions of the Promethean spirit.

Reversing the reasoning, Heidegger was able to say that the hubris of technology is the visible face of the hubris of metaphysics, which in his mind merges with the excesses of rationality, those of instrumental reason. He thought that technology was not a characteristic of modernity among others, like science, capitalism, or democracy. For him, it was the essence of the epoch. He interpreted it as *Gestell*, which one can translate as the "capture" or "enframing" of the energies of Nature. These energies, he says, are no longer "at man's disposal," as one naively believes, but at the disposal of technology itself, whose autonomous power grows exponentially. It is a power in itself, uncontrolled and uncontrollable. Proceeding to draw energy from the depths of the seas, in the sky and soon the stars, technology (the world of "Titans" to use Ernst Jünger's word) has broken the balance of Nature.[18] It uses its power to appropriate. "Neither science, nor politics, still less religion or morality, could master or even temper this technicity that ceaselessly projects its conquests forward."[19]

Who would wield the power of such mastery, if not the very consequences of the hubris of the unlimited? Then the representations of ancient Apollonian wisdom could once again impose themselves.

For the ancient Greeks — Homer, Heraclitus, Aristotle — there exists a cosmic order born of Nature itself. The cosmos finds its source in itself, in a principle of order and beauty that sustains it. This vision of

---

18 An allusion to the ancient divinities, anterior to the Olympian gods, whom the latter, led by Zeus, subjugated at the end of the terrible Titanomachy reported by Hesiod. The Titans were symbols of disordered forces. Their submission allowed the world to be put in order.

19 Jean-François Mattéi, op. cit., pp. 172–173.

the order of the world will later be contested by the biblical interpretation. According to the latter, there exists no rule anterior to the Creator and to his creation. The latter results from Yahweh and nothing else. Yahweh can create, modify, or destroy as he pleases. And it is only by an effect of his good will that he created laws for the universe. This idea of a creative power, anterior and superior to the order of the world, is totally foreign to Homer and the ancient Greeks. The demiurge invoked by Plato only brings to reality what reason holds as possible. He is not the creator; he shows what is.

Athens or Jerusalem

The frontal opposition between these two interpretations was summarized in the 2nd century of our era by Tertullian in a famous formula: "What therefore has Jerusalem to do with Athens, the Church with the Academy, the Christian with the heretic?" When he spoke of Athens, the Christian polemicist was thinking of this philosophical city where Homer's poems had taken their definitive form. A city that, in his eyes, symbolized ancient thought.

If one admits more or less poetically the existence of God, gods, or any other "divine" power merged with the cosmos, the difference between the two conceptions is radical. It lies in this alternative: did God create rules *ex nihilo*, or must he follow pre-existing rules? For Antiquity (Athens), divine will is subordinated to the eternal rules of natural order. For Jerusalem, it represents their independent source. We are therefore in the presence of a clash between two conceptions of the world, a conflict touching on understanding the ultimate laws that govern the universe. This is not a conflict between reason and faith, but a conflict between two different faiths, one in the rules of the ordered cosmos (the tradition of Athens), the other in the sole will of God (the tradition of Jerusalem).

For the family of thought to which Homer, Heraclitus, Plato, and Aristotle belong, the laws that govern the world are eternal (day returns after night, etc.). For that of Moses, Tertullian, and later Mohammed, they come from an eternal God who created the world arbitrarily, by pure will. This notion of a supernatural autonomy of God is at the origin of the idea of autonomy and freedom of men that will emerge much later: "Everything is possible." Such an idea was foreign to the ancient Greeks, for whom "free" means conforming to the rational and eternal order of nature.

Two Visions of the World in Conflict

In accordance with whether one or the other conception dominates, the consequences impose themselves little by little. Today, moderns believe (among other things) that they are spontaneously free to do what they want, to recreate the world and society as they please. "The conceptual model of a spontaneous freedom of man finds its source in the spontaneous freedom of God. Without the archetype of Jerusalem, the idea would not exist today among us."[20] However, modern science has renewed Greek belief. From the moment Galileo had the intuition of the principle of inertia (1604), defined by Newton (1686), the universe was conceived as a great chain of events animated by their own movement. But this belief immediately collided with the idea of a supernatural causality.

In political matters, for example, the question posed in the modern epoch is summated thus: what freedom do men enjoy to live their own life? A tradition of thought that goes from Hobbes to Locke and Burke insists on natural constraints and determinisms weighing on the free will of men. They must discover and observe the law of the world and of life rather than create it.

In the other tradition of thought that goes from Kant to Rousseau and Marx, human free will is, on the contrary, the very source of political legitimacy and good. "It is thus that the paradigm of Jerusalem has been secularized in modernity."

---

20   Boris Dewiel, *Krisis* no. 31 (May 2009).

By an effect of cultural entanglement, where consciousness of scientific causality plays its role, moderns often adhere simultaneously to the idea that there exists a universal order governed by objective laws, and to the idea of spontaneous liberty, which makes us free to do what we want. The philosophical problem of determinism arises at the point where the conflict between the two conceptions of the world is knotted. "To reflect on the question of determinism amounts to experiencing in oneself the shock between Athens and Jerusalem."

The question seems settled. Athens has prevailed over Jerusalem. However, one cannot forget that men remain subject to their dreams and their desires. The cruel experience of communism is not so ancient! It was based on the idea that one is free to fabricate the world as one pleases. Is this idea definitively buried? This is uncertain. Everything must be done so as to not repeat the experience, which pleads in favor of Athens and therefore for the conception of the world embodied by Homer, that of the original European tradition.

This does not merge with ancient mythology and its ancient gods, whether they are sympathetic or not. It is a conception that has a timeless value, just like that of Jerusalem. Simply put, the reflection opened by Tertullian's exclamation proves that the answers to the most current questions and those of the future depend on fundamental choices that traverse time.

CHAPTER III

A DETOUR THROUGH JAPAN

M Y "DETOUR" through Japan owes nothing to any Asian mirage. It is motivated by concern for Europe and its spirit. Through its language, its writing, part of its civilization and customs, Japan is for Europeans a world of otherness, much like China, though in a different manner.[1] And yet, through certain aspects of its history, its refinement, its cult of dignity, and the ethics of its military nobility, it offers astonishing proximities with the best of the European spirit.

Why Compare?

With the first contacts of Christian missionaries in the 17th century, a genuine fascination with Asia, China, and Japan was born in the West among good society. Leibniz bore witness to this in his time. In the 20th century, the crisis of European thought amplified the ancient attraction, which was accompanied by the rejection of how Western culture had become hybrid and infirm. In the eyes of disoriented Europeans, Buddhism and its Zen variant, or Taoism, based on the

---

[1] The idea of this "detour" was partly suggested to me by the method conceived by the philosopher and Sinologist François Jullien in his book of interviews with Thierry Marchaisse, *Penser d'un dehors (la Chine). Entretiens d'Extrême-Occident* (Le Seuil, November 2000). In order to rediscover the authenticity of European thought, François Jullien has undertaken to confront it, including its linguistic structure, with the totally different structure of China, which has developed autonomously, without an inkling of Indo-European languages.

principle of the impermanence of the world, appeared as substitute wisdoms.

The fact is that the "Far Westerners," victims of the intense de-moralization following the two world wars, had often lost faith in the certainties taught to their ancestors. They therefore tended to seek elsewhere what they could no longer find at home. This enthusiasm for exoticism was also based on a self-forgetfulness often bordering on contempt. There were good reasons for this. Among these, the fossilization of our oldest classics by generations of jaded professors. I remember the stupefaction of a classics student at the Sorbonne. Working with sincerity, she was not only thinking about exams, but about what the texts studied could bring her to understand the world and conduct her life. Her professor was surprised and almost indignant to see her take Homer seriously: "But it seems as if for you Homer is alive!" For him, of course, this Homer whose translation he was teaching was dead matter, as were all the ancient authors. This is undoubtedly a major difference with Asia which, except during the Maoist period, never ceased studying its classics in order to draw life lessons from them.

If one wants to reflect in a new way on our way of being Europeans, a detour through Japan proves precious. First of all, it allows us to look differently at our history, our destiny, our values, and our behaviors. Through an exercise in comparative history, it gives our mind the opportunity to breathe. Comparativism modifies the angle of view, it broadens the vision and gives food for different thought.

During the long feudal period, from the 12th to the 19th century, unlike Europe, the Japan of the shoguns lived closed-off to foreigners, voluntarily disinterested in the outside world, concentrating on itself. Yet, it was during this period that its high civilization was perfected as much as the martial ethics of Bushido and *Hagakuré*.[2] The example of Japan shows that one can, following the words of Ortega y Gasset,

---

2   Of this warrior nobility, Akira Kurosawa (1910–1998) gave the most accom-plished cinematographic expression in his film *Kagemusha* (1980).

"command" at home, over oneself, in one's own world, even while turning away from any external conquest. Under certain conditions, it is not impossible to maintain "a regime of high hygiene, of great nobility, of constant stimulants that excite the consciousness of dignity."[3]

The *Waka* of Empress Michiko

Before the Meiji Revolution of 1868 precipitated a forced march into Western modernity, Japan lived concentrated on itself without cultivating the will for external affirmation that was at that time characteristic of European nations. On the other hand, it had brought to a rare point its own way of being, its conquest of itself, like the Greeks before Alexander. It had developed an extremely refined civilization, one which did not exclude cruelty. A civilization punctuated by religious-type rituals that permeated the most minute gestures of life as well as those accomplished during the tea ceremony. This civilization was irrigated by a dynastic permanence going back to the highest antiquity and by the exemplarity of a warrior aristocracy that imposed on itself a strict morality authenticated by recourse to voluntary death. When the trial of 1853 came, the aggressive irruption of the "black ships" of the American Commodore Perry, Japan was not technically prepared. But no country was better prepared mentally to meet the formidable challenge of Western technical power. Nor was any country better prepared to survive the trials of the following century.

The permanence of the Japanese soul can be read today in the short poems (*waka*) of Empress Michiko.[4]

---

3   José Ortega y Gasset, *La Révolte des masses* (Paris: Les Belles Lettres, 2010). Published in 1929, the work was translated into French for the first time in 1937, by Louis Parrot. In this essay, the Spanish philosopher estimated that Europe was entering decadence because it no longer commanded in the world and because it had lost all true aristocracy of merit.

4   A prodigiously gifted young girl of common origin, Michiko was chosen as wife of the Heir Son of the Sun. The origin of the *waka* (short calligraphed poem) is as ancient as that of the country of Yamato, the ancient name of Japan. A part of

Before her husband, Emperor Akihito, 125 emperors of the same lineage had succeeded each other without interruption since the first descendant of the solar goddess Amaterasu, as legend has it. This is enough to make us dizzy, we whose country applies itself in a thousand ways to forget and deny its past.

To penetrate the spirit of Empress Michiko's poems, one can read the last four verses of the *waka* written for the coming-of-age ceremony of Imperial Prince Naruhito:

> *At the threshold of his twenty years, childhood abandoned,*
> *Serene heart of crystal, he will walk henceforth*
> *On the broad and straight path of the glorious ancestors.*
> *Virile prince, he stands there, O my son.*

This was written in February 1980, in a peaceful, democratic, and industrious Japan, supposedly Americanized, 35 years after Hiroshima.

Precisely, for the 50th anniversary of the apocalyptic bombing, in 1995, the empress wrote with infinite restraint the following *waka*:

> *On Hiroshima*
> *struck down fifty years ago,*
> *falls peacefully*
> *the rain*
> *the rain and its sweet scent.*

The previous year, the empress had celebrated on the island of Iwojima the sacrifices of Japanese fighters who had fallen during desperate battles half a century earlier:

> *These places of memory*
> *today peaceful*
> *are filled with water,*

---

the *waka* written by Empress Michiko has been translated into French: *Sé-oto. Le chant du gué, de l'impératrice Michiko du Japon. Anthologie de 53 waka*, translation, notes, chronology, biography, and postface by Tadao Takemoto, with the collaboration of Olivier Germain-Thomas (Paris, éditions Signatura, 2006).

this water that you called in vain,
courageous fighters!

And here again is the brief poem written to commemorate the end of the Second World War:

Gone to what sea, what land
I know not.
They remain invisible,
the noble souls
guardians of the country.

No complaint, no regrets, no tears, although these swell up in the eyes of the reader who is sensitive to the gravity of the words and the evocation of the "noble souls, guardians of the country." These words speak with modest emotion of the eternity and immanence of the Japanese soul.

The Mysteries of Zen

In the Japan of old, the future samurai was subjected from his earliest childhood to a very strict education aimed at teaching him the most perfect self-mastery. His training included intense training in martial arts, governed by the principles of Zen, that particular branch of Buddhism which so fascinates European observers. The latter have applied esoteric interpretations to Japanese martial arts that have often led them astray into ridiculous impasses, adorned with mysterious and empty words: breath, illumination, harmony, sublime truth…

Yet, there are quite few mysteries in the practice of Zen; rather, there are procedures quite similar to those of apprenticeship in trades that exclude reasoning in favor of the education of gesture and the acquisition of reflexes. To train a Japanese cook, one begins by having him wash dishes for months. He is then admitted to a higher level: peeling food. Then will come the moment when he will boil water. Finally, he will be able to plunge rice or some other foodstuff into this water. This is still only a beginning. Years will have already passed, without prior explanations, in absolute submission to the master, repeating gestures until they reach automatic perfection. Whatever flattering artifices surround it, Zen proceeds no differently.

The word *zen* derives from the Sanskrit *dhyâna*, which means meditation. Its teaching is said to have come from India to China around the year 600 and was introduced to Japan in the 12th century, a period which coincides with the establishment of the Japanese version of feudalism. To speak of meditation is improper. This word suggests thought. But there is no thought in Zen; rather, there is a refusal of thought in favor of creating a reflex state through the infinite repetition of the same gestures or the same formulas, a practice found in most religions with invocations or repetitive prayers. Thus, one does not think. On the contrary! One empties the mind. One puts it to rest, which has beneficial effects. One creates emptiness by indefinitely reciting the same prayers or mantras: "Blessed be the name of Buddha [or God]."

Zen is neither a system of ideas, nor a philosophy, nor a religion. It is devoid of dogmas and beliefs, even if one practices it in places of "meditation" or exercise. Its adepts propose the method of the koan, which shocks the Western mind by rejecting any intervention of reason. The oldest Zen poem begins thus: "Conflicts with the just and the unjust, with truth and non-truth, are the disease of the mind." This undoubtedly surprises a rationalist mind accustomed to theoretical jousts. But, by avoiding school debates without answers, this affirmation does not seem devoid of sense.

The Feeling of Nature's Superiority

To a very learned European visitor who came to question him, a Zen master poured him tea and continued after the cup was full until it overflowed. "Master, do you not see that the cup overflows?", cried the visitor. To which the master replied gently: "How do you expect me to be able to teach you something since your mind is like this cup. You came with a mind too full of things. Not to learn, but to criticize, to discuss. So I can teach you nothing."

Such words may shock a Western mind trained in questioning. But it is nonetheless revealing of the non-thought of Zen and its educational method.

This is why, among the samurai, Zen and weapon training are interpenetrated to such an extent that one can no longer discern what belongs to one or the other. Many Zen temples include a meditation hall, the *dojo*, which is used by masters for teaching their martial art. And these masters can be Zen monks, a monastic type very different from Christian monks.

At the root of everything, there predominates in Zen a very strong feeling that beauty, balance, order and harmony reach their perfection in Nature. With some nuances, this feeling was also present in European Antiquity. If one compares humans to other beings of Nature — plants, animals, birds, fish — they often seem like handicapped beings. Nothing is more beautiful and inexplicable than the bursting forth of a flower in spring. The most graceful young girl can hardly rival young does escaping through the woods in an aerial dance. The fastest warrior is slow compared to the lion or leopard.

The Zen explanation: humans are hindered by reason. Reason, far from appearing as superior, is for Zen an obstacle from which it is important to free oneself. Thought interposes itself between the actor and the act. Reason, which Westerners place above all, appears as the rudimentary and coarse stage of perception and action. To act with the lightning ease of the leopard, one must escape thought by acquiring perfect automatisms.

"Never fix one's mind on the point of the saber, the gesture, the eyes of the adversary, or the target," say the master swordsmen. The rule is to see without seeing, to perceive without fixing one's attention, to sense and not to parry an attack. "All art consists in exercising to the point that the adversary becomes transparent, that the intention of his attack is perceived before the attack..." To take a trivial and reductive comparison, it is a bit like what, in their register, experienced automobile drivers or skiing virtuosos achieve. The martial arts, however, are far from being limited to learning reflexes. As the example of *kendo* shows, they include a strong part of religiosity.

The Religious Ritual of Kendo

Young for the most part, kendo practitioners sit upright and silent, helmets and gloves before them. The sun explodes in brief gleams on the masks. Two adversaries rise, their bodies girded with cuirass, faces masked. In hand, they hold the *shinaï* of hard wood. They bow in a deep salute before the gods of the sanctuary.

Before the lightning violence of the assault, kendo — Japanese fencing — is silence, contemplation, concentration. It is a liturgy. The Western spectator perceives in it a dense and impenetrable mystery.

A world separates the fencing practiced in Europe by a minority and kendo, which counts millions of practitioners in Japan. One is a quality sport, the other a martial art, that is to say much more. The first appeals to musculature, suppleness and practical intelligence. The other mobilizes the totality of being, soul as well as body. A fencing assault is a sporting spectacle. A kendo bout is a religious ritual.

This difference is all the more striking since Japan is a model of modernity. Why has the sword lost all symbolic content in Europe and why does the saber remain charged with spirituality in Japan? Why this moral inferiority of Europe compared to Japan? The function of the sword had been just as high in the ancient history of Europe. The attachment of medieval knights to their sword was certainly no less than that of samurai to their saber. It was, however, of another nature. It was not integrated, as for the samurai, into a total morality, a "way" (*do*) as the Japanese say.

While aspiring to an ethics quite its own, the European nobility of sword enjoyed neither the freedom nor the mental tools that would have allowed it to conceptualize its morality. It therefore never had its Bushido.

In the West, from the moment Christianity was adopted as the state religion of the Roman Empire at the end of the 4th century of our era, everything changed. The privilege of moral discourse and knowledge escaped from men of the sword, which did not happen without conflicts. The historian Zoé Oldenbourg highlighted this tension in her book *The Crusades*: "The permanent hostility between clerics and knights that persists throughout the Middle Ages shows well enough to what point the military aristocracy of Western countries was poorly adapted to a religion that was nevertheless theirs for centuries."[5]

The Way of the Samurai

Bearer of an intact and strong tradition, having resisted the subversion of foreign religions, Japan escaped the equivocations that gnawed at the European soul.

The warrior elite of the samurai (*bushi*) was constituted during the troubled period that Japan experienced in the 11th century of our era. It was strengthened in the following century when feudal institutions were formed under the power of the shoguns. In 1192, through war, cunning, and assassination, Yorimoto of the Minamoto clan became the most powerful person in Japan, eclipsing the emperor and taking the title of shogun. Until then, the shogunate had been an exceptional and temporary function entrusted by the emperor to a great lord in situations of peril. Yorimoto made it a permanent institution of government. Despite dynastic changes, the shogunate was maintained until the Meiji Revolution of 1868.

The caste of samurai was composed of warriors in the service of great lords, the *daimyo*. During the long Japanese "Middle Ages," marked by armed struggles between feudal clans, the samurai fought

---

5   Zoé Oldenbourg, *Les Croisades* (Gallimard, 1965; reissued in 2009 in the same publisher's *Folio histoire* collection).

for a *daimyo*, constituting his permanent army. They brought their saber, but also their loyalty, abnegation, and a spirit of discipline without
limit, as illustrated by the authentic story of the 47 ronins.

In March 1701, during a reception organized by the shogun of Edo,
Lord Asano, ignorant of certain court customs, was ridiculed by a
master of ceremonies named Kira, a despicable and corrupt character.
Pushed to the limit, Asano drew his saber and opened the mouth of
the mocker from one ear to the other. Scandal! To shed blood in the
shogun's palace was a crime of lese-majesty. There was no other way
out for Asano than to kill himself following the ritual of *seppuku*.
His domain was seized and his 300 warriors reduced to the state of
ronins — this is what they called warriors without masters, declassed,
devoted to mercenary work, misery, or brigandage.

However, 47 of them, led by Oisjhi Kuranosuké, swore to avenge
their lord. To mislead suspicions, they lived like vagabonds, even
feigning cowardice before Kira's samurai. This lasted almost two years.
Finally, on the night of December 14, 1702, having secretly reunited,
the 47 conspirators launched an assault on Kira's residence. After
having sabered a dozen guards, they found the one they were looking
for. They offered him suicide. Kira remained paralyzed with fear. Cut
down by a saber, his head was placed on Asano's tomb.

The next day, the 47 ronins surrendered as prisoners. The shogun
secretly admired them, but the law was the law. After a year of delib-
erations, the shogunal council invited them to commit ritual suicide.
On February 4, 1703, the 47 ronins gave themselves death by opening
their bellies.

This sacrifice for honor made them forever emblematic heroes. The
sanctuary where they rest continues to be an object of fervent worship
in today's Japan.

Bushido and *Hagakuré*

In 17th-century Japan, which opened the Edo period, the Tokugawa
shoguns had imposed a civil peace throughout the Japanese Empire,

which meant the disappearance of incessant wars between *daimyo*. This pacification rendered the maintenance of numerous samurai armies useless. Those who were deprived of employment were reduced to the state of declassed ronins. It was during this critical period that Yamaga Soko formulated Bushido or "way of the warrior." Rather than a "code," Bushido is a set of precepts. A code implies fixed rules, while the *do*, the "way," is an ethic of life, a school of behavior.

Bushido is in intimate accord with the three spiritual sources of Japan: Shintoism, Zen Buddhism, and Confucianism. It is nourished by the immanence of Shinto, a pantheist religion which was free of any idea of beyond and which associated the cult of ancestors with that of nature. Bushido is inspired by it, also cultivating the Buddhist virtue of detachment and the oblivion of self. But it is a matter of a "Nipponized" Buddhism, rid of non-violence and amended by the wisdom of Zen which teaches self-domination through the practice of a "way," in this case that of various martial arts. Finally, the third source, Confucianism, is a wisdom pertaining to social life. Besides politeness, it teaches that one must assume duties in proportion to his position in the hierarchy.

During his long years of training, the future samurai transforms himself. He frees himself from the fear of death, the ultimate secret of the art of the saber. "I discovered that the Way of the samurai is death," writes Jôchô Yamamoto in the *Hagakuré*, a *savoir-vivre* treatise written in the 17th century for the use of bushi.[6] "If you are required to choose between death and life, choose death without hesitation. Nothing is simpler. Gather your courage and act. According to some, to die without having accomplished one's mission would be to die in vain.

---

6 The text of *Hagakuré* was collected and commented on by Mishima in *Le Japon moderne et l'éthique samouraï* [Modern Japan and the Samurai Ethic] (Gallimard, 1985). Another version of *Hagakuré* was published by Trédaniel editions. The thoughts of samurai Jôchô Yamamoto express harsh criticisms against the peaceful and prosperous Japan of the Tokugawa era (17th century). See also the work by Rinaldo Massi, *Bushido. La Voie des Samouraïs* (Puiseaux: Pardès, 1997).

This is a counterfeit of samurai ethics. All of us prefer to live. There is nothing more natural, therefore, than to seek an excuse to survive. But he who chooses to continue living when he has failed in his mission, he will incur the contempt that goes to cowards and wretches." And Yamamoto insists: "It is necessary to prepare for death every morning and evening, day after day." Thus does one escape the anguish of living and the fear of dying.

If the emblem of the samurai is the cherry blossom that falls before being withered, this is no accident. "Just as the petal of a cherry blossom detaches itself in a ray of morning sun, thus the fearless man must be able to detach himself from existence, silently and with a heart that nothing disturbs."[7]

Discourse and Acts

This detachment is nowhere as brilliant as in the Japanese rite of voluntary death by disembowelment, *seppuku*. According to Chinese anatomical science also adopted by Japan, the part of the belly under the navel (*hara*) is indeed the center of life.

Seppuku was not only a way for the bushi to escape dishonor. It was also the extreme means of displaying their authenticity through a heroic and gratuitous act. They had learned to despise those who speak instead of acting. "They thought that a single act says much more than the longest discourse, for discourse can lie." They believed in the absolute sincerity of the supreme act. They thought that one does not lie before death.

In his essay *Voluntary Death in Japan*, Maurice Pinguet establishes a comparison between the spirit of Japanese nobility of sword and that of European aristocracy in its autumn, between the end of the 16th and the beginning of the 17th century. One does not emerge intact: "While recognizing the same principles of honor and service as the samurai, the sword nobility (French) did not succeed in making its values

---

7   Eugen Herrigel, *Le Zen dans l'art chevaleresque du tir à l'arc* (Paris, Dervy, 1970).

triumph, for since the failure of the Fronde, it is a bourgeois version of Christian beneficence that asserts itself. It will console itself by mocking pharisaism, by laughing at hypocrites and their dupes" — which La Rochefoucauld and the old Fronde nobility, who out of spite took refuge in Jansenism, did. "In Japan, martial ethics succeeded in imposing itself because it put the accent on abnegation [...] He who answers for his honor with his life cannot be suspected of lying. He acts, that is enough... It was the institution of *seppuku* that exempted martial ethics from any utilitarian subordination, that assured its sovereignty over life... Voluntary death came to authenticate with its supreme sanction the whole architecture of martial obligations."[8]

At the end of the Second World War, voluntary death in Japan received an unprecedented consecration when the sacrifice of young kamikazes was demanded. This name *kamikaze* means "divine wind," in memory of a miraculous typhoon that had dispersed a fleet of Mongol invaders in 1281. A special air attack force was constituted in the hope that suicide attacks against American ships could ward off the inevitable. The first attack took place on October 25, 1944. In all, 2,198 pilots sacrificed themselves: 34 American ships were sunk and 288 damaged. However, the enemy naval power was not seriously affected. For his last flight, each kamikaze carried, pressed against him, a traditional saber. Useless death? Perhaps. But certainly not absurd. Only suffered death has no meaning. Willed, it has the meaning one gives it, even when it is without practical utility.

This rhetoric does not leave the European soul insensitive. It makes a secret chord vibrate in it. It is no accident that the ritual suicide of the writer Mishima on November 25, 1970 had such an echo in France and Europe where, formerly, one had also cultivated detachment before death.

---

8   Maurice Pinguet, *La Mort volontaire au Japon* (Gallimard, 1984).

CHAPTER IV

OUR FORGOTTEN MEMORY

THE UPHEAVAL of morals and reference points that has engulfed Europe since the second half of the 20th century has spared no one. The old political religions — those of communism and fascism — have vanished without being replaced. Despite the residual power of the Church, Catholics have suffered from these changes as much as Protestants and the freethinkers of the secular and republican French school.

The End of Old Reference Points

Within the Church, the confusion of many faithful has been aggravated by certain positions of popes and bishops favorable to the incessant flow of extra-European immigration in the name of Christian love and universalism: "All men are brothers." Under Benedict XVI, a pope reputed to be conservative and worthy of respect, the Vatican constantly denounced the timid political measures aimed at limiting the arrival of waves of African and Eastern immigrants. Simultaneously, ostentatious gestures of conciliation were lavished upon Muslims in the name of a common monotheistic origin. Conversely, the resistance efforts of indigenous Europeans, pejoratively called "populists" and criticized for their lack of compassion, were firmly condemned.

With his prophetic prescience, the writer Jean Raspail perfectly expressed one of the ongoing ruptures. Responding to a journalist's questions[1] about the new edition of his novel *The Camp of the Saints*, he said in essence that to repel the invasions of immigrants, one would need to be firm. But, he added, this is impossible. Why? "Because Christian charity forbids it. In a way, Christian charity leads us to disaster!" The one saying this was himself Catholic.

He understood that, to survive, it would be necessary to set aside an important part of the Christian culture that permeates our unconscious and our behaviors. It is by such signs that we measure a historical shift.

More generally, we observe in all European populations the rapid effects of a "gentle" de-Christianization leading them to distance themselves silently, while Africa opens itself ever more to conversions. One consequence is that more and more African priests are called to reinforce the now insufficient indigenous clergies.

Apart from a traditionalist minority that contracts in respectable fidelity to ancient rites and ancient beliefs, contemporary culture — the rational, scientific, hedonistic, ecological, and naturophilic culture of Europe — makes it difficult to accept the old articles of faith. It is difficult to believe in a God of goodness who is the creator and master of a world often so unjust and cruel to the innocent. Hence the evaporation of the idea of salvation and, by reciprocity, of that of hell, the devil, sin, and confession. It becomes difficult to believe in dogmas such as the virginal conception of Jesus, the immortality of the soul, or the "resurrection of the flesh."

Before Immense Perils...

The Biblical text remains widely disseminated, but it is kept at a distance, deprived of its former sacrality. Its readers no longer take as

---

1   Jean Raspail, interview published in *L'Action française 2000* of May 19, 2011, p. 16.

intangible truths what they read with curiosity. Despite reminders to order from above, the old religious practices have been abandoned, replaced by a religion *à la carte*, very distant from the Church's former normative prescriptions regarding sexuality, contraception, abortion, or euthanasia. The depth of the malaise extends to the authority of the magisterium. Since the changes of the 1960s and Vatican II, the cultural fabric on which the Catholic edifice rested has disintegrated. Ample ludic manifestations like World Youth Days have changed nothing. For many "new Christians," won over by ambient hedonism, how can they truly believe that happiness and fulfillment can come only from God and from an "other world" to which it is difficult to give faith?

Within conservative families, there persists an attachment nourished by an anxiety that is probably more social than truly religious. Attachment to the articles of faith, to the apparent security of marriage, to the large family, to the traditional education of children, favors this fidelity. Elsewhere, we see the birth of countless religions, sects, or replacement "wisdoms." Different versions of the "New Age" or Buddhism attract former faithful. They reconcile a vaporous supernatural, a compassion in accord with Christian sensibility, and great liberality in matters of morals and sexual morality. Due to the demographic and cultural pressure exerted by immigration in the suburbs on the isolated youth and lost "Gauls," we also see multiplying conversions to Islam in both sexes. Finally, extending silently and without fanfare, we see the perception of a presence in the world of the immanentist type, ignoring the perspectives of a beyond.

Taking note of these upheavals, I have given a new meaning to the word "tradition" in a book that has made history for some.[2] This book was born from my anxieties before immense perils, but also from my faith in our European homeland's capacities for survival and renaissance after the catastrophes of the 20th century. In the very title of

---

2   Dominique Venner, *Histoire et tradition des Européens*, 2nd ed. (Le Rocher, 2004).

this book, I intentionally used the word "tradition" in the singular. My goal was not to enumerate various traditions in the usual sense of the word. I was no more interested in artistic or political traditions than in the tradition of good drinking and good eating or in the tradition of critical thinking… Tradition as I understand it in a new and even "revolutionary" way is not a set of customs and practices, a certain way of acting or thinking transmitted by education or usage. It is not what opposes modernity. It is even less a set of universal and supernatural principles imagined by gnostics. It is not the nostalgic memory of a vanished Golden Age. Tradition as I understand it is not the past, but on the contrary, that which does not pass and which always returns under different forms. It designates the essence of a civilization over the very long term, that which resists time and survives the disturbing influences of religions, fashions, or imported ideologies.

Historical Variations and Permanences

High European civilization cannot be confused with the transitory society in which we live at the moment of my writing. The current cosmopolitan system is a product of European decline, American hegemony, and market capitalism. It is in no way identical to our perennial civilization. This must be sought elsewhere, in the best of what it has bequeathed to us.

Great civilizations are not regions on a planet, they are different planets.[3] Like other civilizations — those of China, India, or the Semitic East — ours is of immemorial origin. It plunges far into prehistory. It rests on a specific tradition that merges with the spirit of the *Iliad*, traversing time under changing appearances. According to Fernand Braudel's definition: "A civilization is a continuity which, when it changes, even as profoundly as a new religion might imply, incorporates ancient values that survive through it and remain its substance."[4]

---

3   This formula is by René Marchand.

4   Fernand Braudel, *Écrits sur l'histoire* (Flammarion, 1969).

This substance is made up of living aesthetic and spiritual values that structure our behaviors and nourish our representations. If, for example, simple sexuality is universal in the same way as the action of nourishing oneself, love expresses itself differently in each civilization, just as there are different representations of femininity, pictorial art, and music. These are the reflections of a certain spiritual morphology, transmitted undoubtedly as much by atavism as by acquisition. These specificities make us what we are, like no others. They constitute our perennial tradition, a unique way of being women and men in the face of life, death, love, history, destiny.

Our tradition survives in our unconscious while we have partly forgotten it, under the effect of very ancient fractures that have broken our memory. Under the effect also of belief in the universal vocation of our modernity, inherited from Christian messianism and that of the Enlightenment.

To be convinced of this, it suffices to observe with fresh eyes what the variations and historical permanences show us.

No century ends as it began. This is true for Antiquity as well as for periods called modern. Less than 20 years separate the destruction by the Persians of the Greek cities of Ionia from the revenge at Salamis and Plataea of the cities coalesced around Athens and Sparta. Witness to the last century before our era, Sallust was convinced that Rome had perished before his eyes in the corruption of morals and the horrors of civil war. A few decades later began the prosperous reign of Augustus and the founding of the Empire. At the beginning of our 16th century, the lower clergy was favorable to the Reformation. Sixty years later, it had become its worst enemy, providing the thick battalions of the League. From century to century, one could multiply examples of all kinds, including for China, that falsely immobile power.

The unexpected is a constant in the history of states and nations. On the other hand, on the completely different scale of civilizations, it is less the unexpected that dominates than the long permanences, under the appearance of changes. Civilizations are realities of very long duration. Contrary to Paul Valéry, they are not "mortal" on the scale of an individual life. Their pathologies do not have the irreversible character imagined by Spengler. And if major catastrophes are capable of destroying them, like the Mayas, the Aztecs, or the Incas, these are exceptions. So great is the survival capacity of civilizations. Most often, what one interprets as a death is a dormancy. It is astonishing to observe, for example, that after a coma of several centuries, the Aztec people experienced a sort of resurrection in the last decades of the 20th century. What perishes are the apparent forms, such as political or religious institutions. But the roots of civilizations are practically indestructible as long as the people who were their matrix have not disappeared.

The Perenniality of Mother Civilizations

The Greco-Roman part of European civilization seemed to die when Christianity was imposed. But an unconventional and "traditionist" gaze will spot the ancient survivals in the West during the Christian centuries, to the point that they would experience prodigious intellectual, spiritual, and artistic renaissances starting in the 15th century and well beyond.

It has also been said that the Renaissance had placed at the heart of Christendom a pagan civilization that was its negation. In reality, this civilization, born in Greece on the Hellenic branch of the Western Indo-Europeans, then surviving in Rome, was never really uprooted. In the West, the Church poured itself into the imperial mold from which it drew its strength, the philosophy of Plato and Aristotle offering it its rational justifications. Its moral teaching was partly modeled on that of the Stoics. And to incorporate the immense people of the countryside, it took over the ancient ritual festivals, the cult of sacred springs, and that of familiar divinities to which it gave the names of saints.

It was the same everywhere else. New religions have rarely replaced or suppressed the old ones. They have been the vehicle by which civilizations have survived the ruin of exhausted structures. Even Islam, the most violent of new beliefs and the most closed to compromises, did not escape this rule. The Umayyads moved their capital from Medina to Damascus, a Hellenistic and Byzantine city. Of Theodosius' cathedral, they made a great mosque. Its Byzantine architecture served as a model throughout the Arab world, including for the Dome of the Rock in Jerusalem. Overthrowing the Umayyads in 750, the Abbasids wanted to restore the purity of Islam. But, having made Iran the center of their power, they unknowingly embraced its civilization. While building Baghdad and relying on high Persian functionaries, the Abbasid caliphs adopted the etiquette and rules of the ancient Sassanid empire, reviving its art and literature.

Civilization, culture, and tradition are neighboring notions to the point of being interchangeable in common language. Culture is first in the chronological order of foundation. It relates to the permanence of deep mentalities. It is creative of meaning. Civilization is a culture that has received a historical form, creative of a set of proper qualities in the material, intellectual, artistic, and moral order. Tradition is the soul of a culture and a civilization. One can speak of mother civilizations and daughter civilizations. Thus, Chinese civilization is the mother of several secondary civilizations of East Asia, such as the Korean, Japanese, or Vietnamese. Sanskrit civilization radiated from the plains of the Ganges to Indonesia and Cambodia. Emerging from the Arabian Peninsula, Muslim civilization also influenced very vast spaces, from the Mediterranean to the Indian subcontinent and well beyond. Similarly, Greek civilization, born with Homer, is the mother civilization of all Europe, from ancient Rome to the Celtic and Germanic kingdoms of the Middle Ages, then to modern nations.

Like cultures, civilizations are irreducible to one another. They are like persons having their own destinies. In space, they extend beyond the limits of states and nations. Being realities of long duration, they survive political, economic, or religious upheavals. They surpass in longevity all other collective realities. They have eternity for them. So it is with European civilization, despite what today disfigures it to the point that one would almost imagine it dead.[5]

Some Celebrated Precedents

Certain unexpected examples of returning to ancient representations, freed from Christianity, have celebrated and well-documented precedents. In Germany, Goethe, Nietzsche, or Heidegger; in Spain, Ortega y Gasset; in Italy, Croce, Pareto, Marinetti, and Julius Evola. In France, in the contemporary period, one thinks of the explicit positions of Hippolyte Taine, Anatole France, Ernest Renan, Fustel de Coulanges, Maurice Barrès, Thierry Maulnier, Jacques Laurent, Lucien Rebatet, Emil Cioran. But one can dwell for a moment on the examples of Montherlant, Maurras, Céline, and, to a lesser extent, Marshal Lyautey, who all left written testimonies to which one can refer.

Henry de Montherlant reported more than once, notably in his essay *The Thirteenth Caesar*,[6] the shock that was reading *Quo Vadis* at eight years old. The Christian part of Sienkiewicz's novel hardly impressed him. He was accustomed to Christian characters. His religious instruction books were full of them. What he had no idea of was pagan society, and even less the critique of Christianity. Let one imagine the

---

5   In Antiquity, the name Europe, used by Herodotus and Hecataeus of Miletus, had a particularly geographical significance. The first known document where the word Europeans is used to designate a people, in this case the Franks, dates from the Battle of Poitiers, in 732, during which Charles Martel broke the Muslim advance. The account of a contemporary Iberian chronicler, known as the anonymous of Córdoba, opposes on one side "the Arabs" and on the other "the Europeans" (*europenses* in Latin). He speaks neither of Christians nor of Muslims, a fact to be noted. Did Europe become aware of itself during this major event? The question remains open. Cf. Anonymous of Córdoba, Latin text J. Tailhan (1885) translated in Ch.-M. De La Roncière, R. Delort and M. Rouche, *L'Europe au Moyen Âge* (Paris, Armand Colin, 1969), vol. 1, pp. 137–139.

6   Henry de Montherlant, *Le Treizième César* (Gallimard, 1970).

seizure, or as he writes, the stupefaction of an eight-year-old child, surrounded by undisputed Catholicism, when he comes upon phrases like: "Leave me in peace with your Christians […] I tell you they are fools, that you feel it yourself, and that if your nature repugns to follow their doctrine, it is precisely because you vomit at their imbecility" (Petronius to Vinicius). And again, when Petronius is told of "love" in the Christian sense of the word, love for one's neighbor: "Where will I find this love that is not in my heart?"

To crown the unexpected, "my anti-Christianity," comments Montherlant, "was revealed to me by my mother and my grandmother, good Christians if ever there were, donors of the book, and of a book reputed to be edifying." He adds that the novel had the same effect on his friend Faure-Biguet, raised in a family as Catholic as his own.

Here, then, are two boys from excellent families to whom the reading of a Christian novel suddenly revealed that they were different, a conviction which they upheld thereafter until death. In Montherlant, this did not contradict his admiration for the noble natures who populated the elite of Catholicism and inspired, for example, his *Port Royal* (1954).

Examples of returns to the sources are not lacking. The 19th century knew that of Gérard de Nerval through poetry, or those of Renan and Loisy through philosophy. One was a brilliant seminarian, while the second, his junior, taught the Holy Scriptures at the Catholic Institute of Paris. In his genre, Charles Maurras is equally emblematic.

The Ancient Paganism of Charles Maurras

His father having died prematurely, it was the influence of a very pious mother that was exerted on the little Provençal. In this supremely intelligent child, who dreamed of being a sailor, the precocious reading of the *Odyssey* was a first revelation. At 15, as a student at the Catholic college of Aix-en-Provence, he was struck by deafness. Abbé Penon, a Provençal, future bishop of Moulins, became his tutor and spiritual

director. He saw his task compromised by the evolution of his pupil
and the intractable autonomy of his spirit. He had introduced the
child to knowledge of ancient letters, which gradually turned him
away from Christianity. Now agnostic, the young Maurras dropped
his studies and went to Paris, swearing to make a career in journalism
and literature. He was 17.

After a brief season of literary anarchism, nostalgia for his native
Provence and ancient luminaries brought him back to Homer. In
November 1894, he published his first book, *The Path of Paradise*, a
collection of philosophical tales. In the preface to this reverie, he confessed his desire to castigate Biblical Christianity, which he believed
was destructive of pagan and classical harmony. The work was reprinted in 1921, purged of what might shock the Catholic public. Having
founded in the meantime the newspaper and league of *Action française*, Maurras found himself indeed prisoner of a majority Catholic
and conservative public.

In the spring of 1896, at 18, he had been sent to Athens as a journalist to cover the Olympic Games. These Games were the first to be
organized since their prohibition, 15 centuries earlier, by the Christian
emperor Theodosius. The young man was exhilarated by this journey.
He brought back *Anthinéa*, published in 1901. This very pagan work
contained anti-Christian pages that were expurgated in later editions.

His correspondence with Abbé Penon, however, bears witness to
what his intimate convictions were.[7] Everything is summarized in his
letter of June 28, 1896: "I return from Athens more distant, more of an
enemy of Christianity than before. Believe me, it is there that the perfect men lived…" After having evoked Sophocles, Homer, and Plato, he
concludes: "I return from Athens as a pure polytheist. What was vague
and confused in my thought has become precise with brilliance. I flee
the idea of the infinite, a Semitic, Hebraic idea, a contradictory idea
from Asia, from the barbarians. I no longer want to think of anything

---

7   *Correspondance entre Charles Maurras et l'abbé Penon* (1883–1928), presented by
    Axel Tisserand under the title *Dieu et le roi* (Privat, 2007).

but the perfect and the pure..." Until his death in 1928, Abbé Penon tried to make Maurras return from this conversion to "paganism." In vain.

He obtained only concessions of pure form, but also the unusual argument by which Maurras, in the name of the ancient political alliance of Throne and Altar, displayed his veneration for the Catholic Church, cornerstone of social order in his eyes, isolated from a Christianity judged pernicious...

A primarily political mind, Maurras did not intend to make himself a spiritual or religious reformer. He locked in his heart the revolts and intimate convictions that were no longer expressible without peril. The shadow of a rallying, wrested on his deathbed, changed nothing. At the moment of dying, the amiable Jean de La Fontaine had been victim in his time of even worse harassments.[8] The model of exhortations used to make him yield was found in Pascal, determined to despair his readers in order to remove their hope of finding other recourse to their infirmity than those of his religion.

Céline's Virulent Polemic

Considered the greatest French writer of the 20th century, a renovator of language and style, inhabited by a sort of prophetic delirium, Louis-Ferdinand Destouches, Céline in literature, constitutes another example of radical insubordination. Gravely wounded during the first combat of 1914, he was decorated and discharged. Having undertaken medical studies, he defended his thesis on the life and work of Dr. Semmelweis in 1924. Entered into the Health Service of the League of Nations, he was sent on missions to the US, Europe, and Africa until 1927. Five years later, he published *Journey to the End of the Night*, immediately hailed as a major literary work. Just like Léon Daudet in *Action française*, the left intelligentsia reserved a warm welcome for

---

8   Jean de La Fontaine, *Lettres à sa femme, voyage de Paris en Limousin*. Preface by Michel Mourlet (Paris, Valmonde-Trédaniel, 1995).

an author who seemed to belong to them, but the writer-doctor was refractory to all regimentation. The publication of *Mea Culpa* (1936) following his trip to the USSR showed that he had not been duped by the Soviet paradise. This book consummated his divorce with a left dominated by communists.

Sensing a new war coming, Céline attributed responsibility to a Jewish conspiracy. In quick succession, he published two pamphlets that suddenly made him appear as a rabid antisemite: *Trifles for a Massacre* (1937) and *School for Corpses* (1938). Vituperating against war and the coming carnage, he denounced in his fashion "the coalition of Anglo-Saxon capitalism, Stalinism, and the Jewish lobby" whose objective (according to him) was to send French youth to massacre in a Franco-German war in which it would not intervene until the sacrificed combatants' exhaustion.[9]

In a rather different genre, Céline published in 1941 a new pamphlet, *Fine Mess*, undoubtedly the only one of his works illuminated by a light halo of hope. Alongside a famous tirade on "Labiche communism," he delivered a poetic meditation on the spirit of France, written in the style of 15th-century ballads and *virelais*, not without some quite unjust swipes at Montaigne.

This time, this curious book, where antisemitism, though present, is quite muted, delivered a furious message against Christian preaching, the ultimate recourse of the Vichy regime he despised: "Propagated to virile races, to detested Aryan races, the religion of 'Peter and Paul' admirably accomplished its work, it turned them into mandingos, into sub-men from the cradle, subjected peoples, hordes intoxicated with Christic literature, imbeciles madly driven to the conquest of the Holy Shroud, magic hosts, forever abandoning their Gods of blood, their Gods of race... Hence the sad truth, the Aryan has never known how to love, adore anything but the god of others, never had his own religion, white religion... What he adores,

---

9   Pierre Monnier, "*Céline et les têtes molles,*" *Bulletin célinien* (Brussels, 1998).

his heart, his faith were furnished to him completely by his worst enemies..." Albeit in different words, Nietzsche didn't say anything different.

The work was banned by Vichy services in the Southern zone and aroused the strongest reservations from the Propaganda Abteilung...

Lyautey's Rationalism

With Hubert Lyautey, illustrious marshal, it is a completely different register that expresses itself. Like Montherlant or Maurras, Lyautey had received the most Catholic education. As a young officer, several times he made retreats at the Grande Chartreuse while experiencing serious philosophical doubts. In 1884, a period of great Catholic reconquest, writing to his friend Antonin de Margerie, he confessed: "I no longer have faith."[10] Why? His reason had made him doubt. His reason alone, which is little. Hubert Lyautey ceased to believe in the Christian mysteries of Salvation or Incarnation, as in those of an all-powerful creator God of an evil world. These mysteries offended his reason. However, he did not return to sources anterior to Christianity, for lack of knowing them. He was not aware of belonging to a very ancient tradition that it was necessary to rediscover, and to construct his existence in accord with his nature. This is a great difference with Montherlant, Maurras, and, to a certain extent, Céline. They had not left Christianity to fall into the void. They were not concerned with the anxiety of nothingness arising from the death of the Christian God, as Nietzsche said.

They had left Christianity, as one frees oneself from a foreign system, to rediscover the spiritual universe of their origins. A universe that had begun before them and would continue after. This ancient spiritual world was rich, harmonious, and satisfying. It brought answers to all the essential questions of life and death. Hubert Lyautey

---

10   André Le Révérend, *Un Lyautey inconnu. Correspondance et journal inédit, 1874–1934* (Perrin, 1980).

was not armed to do this work by himself. Like most rationalists, from his rupture, he had to live in cruel spiritual aridity. And since he felt a need for spirituality, this nothingness finally became unbearable to him. In his old age, no longer able to bear it, he forced himself to believe again, so as to escape the void. For lack of anything better, he then inclined toward what he knew. He therefore returned to the practices of his youth, abandoned long ago by the intellectual refusal of mysteries and dogmas judged absurd. Priests helped him in this return. He became again what he had never ceased to be at bottom, a conventional Christian tormented by reason.

The counter-example of Hubert Lyautey is enlightening. By contrast, it allows us to better understand what the return to tradition can mean for Europeans.

An Immense Historical Fracture

Hubert Lyautey had not been interested in the origins of the religion from which he had detached himself in his mature age. It is, nevertheless, a capital history that is little-known. It concerns all Europeans, but it has not been taught to them. This history is that of the unexpected adoption by the Roman Empire, at the end of the 4th century, of a cult that was foreign to it and from which everything subsequently proceeded. One cannot understand this immense event if one neglects the upheavals provoked in the Roman world by the conquests that led to the formation of a cosmopolitan empire.

At the very beginning of the 2nd century, the poet Juvenal had sounded the alarm: "*In Tiberium defluxit Orontes*" ("Into the Roman Tiber flows the Eastern Orontes"). Rome would die from its conquests and the corrupting riches of the Semitic East. The warrior republic had been transformed into a brothel for exotic nabobs. The golden slippers had replaced the boots, so to speak. Rome was no longer in Rome. Drawing on immense erudition, Renan said everything on this subject in *Marcus Aurelius and the End of the Ancient World*. In the

3rd century, there reigned various Berber emperors, Syrian empresses, Heliogabalus, a tinsel emperor, weak and debauched, who introduced his Asian gods into the City. Later came Emperor Philip the Arab… Despite harsh military reactions, the habit was taken of governing in the Oriental manner — despotism, corruption, and cruelty.

A vigorous health transfusion had nevertheless begun in Romanized Gaul with the Celts (Gauls), then the Germanics. Despite Tacitus who admired them, the Germanics have long been described as hirsute savages. After many other historical works, the exhibition organized in Venice at the Palazzo Grassi in 2008, "Rome Saved by the Barbarians," rendered them justice. Contradicting the legend, the learned commissioners of this exhibition recalled that Rome had not been put to death by the Germanic "great invasions" of the 4th century. It had even been saved by the contribution of blood and vigor that was at the origin of the Frankish, Burgundian, or Visigothic kingdoms, protecting it from other Barbarians, such as the Huns or the Arabs. More than two thousand pieces and works of art gathered at the Palazzo Grassi showed the true face of those who founded medieval Europe. Their assimilation to Romanity was a success. This had begun with war, as always between great peoples. The legions struck hard and were sometimes massacred themselves, as at Teutoburg in the year 9 of our era. Then, the fusion with Rome was accomplished gradually, favored undoubtedly by the same Indo-European origin and shared values. From the 3rd century, several Germanics (Franks, Visigoths) had become consuls and generals. Stilicho, a Vandal, defended Rome against the Ostrogoths before marrying the daughter of Emperor Honorius. According to the claims of school history, Antiquity was undoubtedly already dead when Odoacer deposed the last emperor of the West in 476. But at the same instant was born medieval Europe, which implicitly took up the heritage of the Greco-Roman world, in the context of a new state religion whose adoption had been favored by Constantine.

A Universal Church for a Universal Empire

The birth of this religion did not happen in an instant, and its diffusion did not proceed without resistance. It took three centuries to establish itself, the span of time that separates us from the end of the reign of Louis XIV. The small dissident Jewish sect at its origins had become in the meantime a priestly institution with universal pretension that Saint Paul had opened to all the uncircumcised (the "Gentiles"), a religion that henceforth wanted to be that of all men.

This project of Christian universality coincided with the universal ambition of imperial Rome. It was even its copy, which influenced it and then favored its adoption as state religion after periods of conflict and despite constant and unusual heresies. For an empire with universal vocation, a religion that wanted to be that of all men was better suited than the religion of the indigenous gods of the ancient Roman city. One rarely thinks of this capital reality.

Everything politically pleaded in favor of this adoption, and Christian apologists did not fail to emphasize it.[11] Unlike the ancient civic religion, the new one was individual and personal. Through prayer, each faithful entered into an imploring relationship with the new God.

This one did not oppose imperial universality. We know the saying: "Render unto Caesar what is Caesar's, and unto God what is God's." In principle, the two universes of Caesar and God were separate but complementary. Through the voice of Saint Paul, the nascent Church had even justified in advance the authority of the Caesars: "All power comes from God" (Romans 13).

Except for demanding the monopoly of faiths, the new religion was mute in politics. In this regard, the sick Empire of the time could not wish for anything better than a religion ready to serve it by unifying all

---

11   On the evolution of the Church in the first centuries, one may consult the first four chapters of Jean-Pierre Moisset, *Histoire du catholicisme* (Flammarion, "Champs," 2010).

peoples and all races in the adoration of the same God without ethnic attachment. On the condition, however, that it be recognized to the exclusion of all others. From this God, said to be creator of heaven and earth, power could even draw new legitimacy after having made its cult obligatory. Emperor Constantine, imitated in this by his successors in the East (Byzantium), was quite determined to intervene in the affairs of a Church he wanted submissive, and to bring order to theological disputes pregnant with heresies and divisions. His authority thus imposed itself at the Council of Nicaea (325), which established the foundations of Catholic orthodoxy by giving dogmatic foundation to the mystery of the divine trinity.

The revolution of Constantine and his successors had immense and unforeseeable effects on European becoming. The adoption of Christianity initiated by the Edict of Milan (313) lifted the ancient prohibitions and favored the Church in a thousand ways. This revolution provoked resistances to which the young emperor Julian, Constantine's nephew, who reigned from 361 to 363, testified. After his death, his successors resumed with Christianity, which became state religion under Theodosius by the edicts of 391 and 392. These reinforced the privileges of the new religion and prohibited traditional cult under penalty of death.[12]

---

12   On the resistances of Roman tradition, one may consult Ernest Renan, *Histoire des origines du christianisme*, Book VII, *Marc Aurèle et la fin du monde antique* (Robert Laffont, "Bouquins," 1995); Louis Rougier, *Celse contre les chrétiens* (Copernic, 1977); Pierre Chuvin, *Chronique des derniers païens* (Les Belles Lettres, 1990); Ramsay MacMullen, *Christianisme et paganisme du IVe au VIIIe siècle* (Les Belles Lettres, 1998); Peter Brown, *Pouvoir et persuasion dans l'Antiquité tardive, vers un empire chrétien* (Le Seuil, 1998); Paul Veyne, *Quand notre monde est devenu chrétien*, 312–394 (Albin Michel, 2007); Lucien Jerphagnon, *Julien dit l'Apostat* (Tallandier, 2008); Guy Rachet, *Les Racines de notre Europe sont-elles chrétiennes et musulmanes?* (Jean Picollec, 2011).

A Formidable Power Machine

The new religion was initially established on the apocalyptic certainty of an imminent end of the world and on the promise that only the faithful would be saved. Other religious sects have used the same stratagem, but in undoubtedly less favorable circumstances. After Theodosius' edicts, imitation of "Christian" emperors was imposed. To careerist incitement were added social and physical constraints. The former persecuted became persecutors and remained so for a long time. To impose itself, the new religion originally lacked the intellectual and liturgical instruments of Greco-Roman paganism: philosophy, poetry, rhetoric, theater, architecture, painting, music, all condemned up to then by Christianity.[13]

Pressed by the necessity to compose with a refined civilization, ecclesiastical elites were constrained to convert a large part of the beliefs and rites belonging to pagan tradition (from solstice festivals to the cult of saints who took the place of the familiar lesser gods). At the initiative of Gregory the Great (pope from 590 to 604), the new religion slipped into ancient customs and the great pagan festivals were aggregated to the Christian calendar. Miraculous springs were also Christianized, as well as sacred stones and places of worship. Not without difficulty or resistance, the polytheistic philosophical system was integrated into the new religion, which found itself transformed. Christian authors like Origen, Tertullian, Augustine, Ambrose, and their successors thus nourished themselves on Greek Neoplatonism before criticizing it.

In fact, the link with ancient thought was never broken. It has thus been said that Boethius (c. 478–525) was the educator of the Middle

---

13   It is by lexical simplification that I use the word "paganism" which is, as we know, of much later Christian origin. During the Middle Ages, all humans who were not Christians were denounced as "pagans" (from *paganus*: peasant, implicitly a fool). In the *Song of Roland*, Muslims are called pagans. In the accepted usage, "pagans" are all those who, by fidelity to ancient European cults, reject the various monotheisms.

Ages. Born into a noble Roman family, he made a career in the high imperial administration under Theodoric (425–526), the Ostrogothic king who tried to restore the Western Empire from his capital, Ravenna, where his mausoleum is preserved. Accused of conspiracy in favor of the Byzantines, Boethius was exiled near Pavia before being put to death on Theodoric's order. During his forced exile, he wrote his major work, *The Consolation of Philosophy* (*De consolatione philoso-phiae*), which was one of the most read and commented upon books by medieval clerics from the 9th century. In this great book, where prose and poetry alternate, Boethius meditates on the thought of Plato and Seneca, also bequeathing to the following centuries the translation of a large part of Aristotle's *Organon*.[14]

The Christianity of the 4th–5th centuries also had to compose with the interpretation of Jewish Scriptures in a Hellenized milieu rubbed with Greek rationalism. The history of innumerable heresies shows that no religion in the world has known such a variety of interpreta-tions with cruelly conflictual consequences. The religion of love then produced among its own an inexpiable hatred over questions that seem futile or incomprehensible to our eyes.[15] It was in the blood and ashes of heresiarchs, amid terrible tearings, that the official doctrine was thus constructed.

To understand how this adventure lasted (setting aside the in-terventions of Providence, which the historian is not one to judge), one must take into account that from its adoption as imperial reli-gion, nascent Christianity became a formidable power machine. Moreover, like all salvation religions, it had an essential superiority over political imperium. Unlike princes, cities, emperors, it was not subject to the test of results. This religion promised nothing on earth and everything in another world of which it was the sole judge and

---

14 Pierre de Courvelle, *Les Lettres grecques en Occident, de Macrobe à Cassiodore* (De Boccard, 1948).

15 Pierre de Meuse, *Histoire des hérésies. Des origines du christianisme à la Réforme* (éditions Trajectoire, 2010).

interpreter. One can also add that with the founding principle of Fault (original sin), coupled with the privilege the Church had of remitting sins, Christianity implicitly flattered humans' bad inclinations, since these were forgivable, contrary to Stoicism, which excused no one from their responsibilities. This was undoubtedly a secret seduction of Christianity: to have mixed a discourse of moral rigor and an accommodating practice. Thus, the morality of fault and sin did not lack assets to evict the former, more demanding ethic of honor and pride. Yet, we see Saint Augustine deploy great dialectical efforts in *The City of God* to ruin the admiration traditionally given to the Stoic heroism of young Lucretia and Cato of Utica.

In the eyes of the "old Romans," as testified by the discourse of Celsus or that of Emperor Julian, Christianity was initially perceived as resting on a ridiculous fable. It was impious, scandalous, and even revolutionary ("the first shall be last"). Then, having become the state religion imposed to the exclusion of all others, adorned with the attractions of power, revered consequently by all good and necessarily conformist society, except for a few rebels, it appeared over the centuries (and still today for conservative Catholics) as being the very expression of what they felt as tradition, after having been its absolute negation.

The Pact of Clovis

The new imperial religion since the end of the 4th century, Christianity imposed itself as the Empire was about to disappear in the West in 476. *A contrario*, the Empire, it is often forgotten, would maintain itself in the East for ten more centuries, until the taking of Constantinople by the Turks in 1453. The consequences of this partition of the former imperium profoundly affected the history of Europe and that of the Church. In the East, the latter remained subject to the temporal authority of the emperor, as Constantine had wanted. Thus were born both the Caesaro-Papism of Byzantium and then the autocephalous Orthodox confessions. Conversely, in the West, the disappearance of imperial authority left an immense field open to the Church and to new political forms.

When the last phantom emperor of the West disappeared in 476, the Church had paradoxically become the ultimate imperial institution. It did not only monopolize spiritual power. For nearly a century, it also held the essentials of administrative and territorial power. By decision of Theodosius (edict of 392), recruitment for high administration had become exclusively Christian. Thus demanded the logic of state religion desired by the Church and adopted by emperors, apostates from ancient cults, at the risk of attracting many opportunists and hypocrites. But such is always the case in all religions associated with political power.

In the great Gaul of the 5th century, Romanized for a long time and in the process of being "Franconized," bishops had become the local holders of most powers and riches of the Empire, except for the power of arms and that of political sovereignty. This sovereign power was taken up by Clovis when he, already strong from the military and demographic weight of his Franks, concluded a pact of alliance with the episcopate of Gaul, strange heir to the incomparable Roman power and its prestige. This pact was sanctioned by the conversion of the Frankish king.[16] For analogous reasons, over the following centuries, Clovis was imitated by all Germanic or Slavic kings, until then pagan, and the founders of all European kingdoms, from Norway to Kievan Russia (which adopted Byzantine Orthodoxy due to a geopolitical context favorable to Constantinople).

---

16   The exact date of Clovis' conversion is disputed (496 or 499). On this period, one may consult Patrick J. Geary, *Naissance de la France. Le monde mérovingien* (Flammarion, "Champs," 1989). One may also refer to the dossier of *La Nouvelle Revue d'Histoire* no. 43 (July–August 2009), *"Les racines de l'Europe. D'Homère à Clovis."*

The Incongruous Heiress of Ancient Rome

It is important to specify, however, that all Germanic kings thought themselves descendants of one or another of their gods (Thor, Odin, etc.). Their conversion did not make them renounce this belief, which was inscribed in their tradition. They only Christianized it. Thus was established (or maintained) the principle of European monarchies of "divine right," to which the Church added its own consecration and Biblical interpretation so as to remain master of the game.

Without anyone finding fault, except for the faithful of ancient cults, which were now prohibited, and even before the new Western Empire was founded by Charlemagne (in 800), followed by the Holy Roman Germanic Empire by Otto the Great (in 962), the Church had thus become the heiress of ancient Roman power, its splendor and riches, as attested by, among other things, the symbolic choice of Rome as seat of the future papacy. However, the spiritual and political heritage of the Roman Empire would subsequently be fiercely disputed between the pope, the (Germanic) emperor, and national kings who, imitating Philip IV the Fair, wanted to be "emperor in their kingdom." In the name of their own "divine right," they often contested the spiritual supremacy to which the pope pretended.[17]

For several centuries, Europeans were thus torn between ancient cities, the Holy Empire, and the Church itself.[18] The latter enjoyed spiritual power (monopoly over sacred word and the power of excommunication), but it aspired to more. This was the source of all conflicts.[19] This was also the cause of an immense tearing of minds from

---

17 *La Nouvelle Revue d'Histoire*, dossier no. 63 (November–December 2012), "*Le conflit du Trône et de l'Autel.*"

18 Pierre Manent, *Les Métamorphoses de la cité. Essai sur le dynamisme de l'Occident* (Flammarion, 2010).

19 One may consult on this subject Sylvain Gouguenheim, *La Réforme grégorienne. De la lutte pour le sacré à la sécularisation du monde* (Temps Présent, 2010). See also Bernard Fontaine, "*Le choc des deux glaives au Moyen Âge*" in *La Nouvelle Revue d'Histoire* no. 51, p. 15.

which Europe has never truly recovered. "A dreadful disorder," specifies philosopher Pierre Manent, "a conflict of authorities and loyalties," and a conflict of words and actions.

"Christianity has introduced an unprecedented gap between what men do and what they say."[20] Why? Because "the Christian Word asks men to love what they naturally hate — their enemies — and to hate what they naturally love — themselves." Commenting on this reflection, Pierre Manent lengthily cites *The City of God*. We know the central argument: "Two loves made two cities, love of self to the contempt of God made the earthly city, and love of God to the contempt of self made the celestial city." This founding book gave the faithful the model of the City of God so that they would turn away from the seductions and sins of the earthly city that had been the delights of pagans. The reversal of perspective imposed by Augustine and his successors had profoundly disturbing effects over the long epochs during which the Christian word enjoyed absolute authority.

The Lesson of Regensburg

Thus, from the 4th century of our era, following great and unforeseen historical events, an exotic cult had become the obligatory religion of a cosmopolitan Empire that had nothing Roman but the name. And yet, the memory of the grandeur of ancient Rome never faded even while its temples were demolished to build the edifices of the new cult. It is even (in a supreme paradox) on this memory that the Church was able to found its own power. At all times, however, men and women of Europe have seen awakening in them, more or less consciously, the thirst for their primordial tradition. This resurrection has always been accomplished unexpectedly, as in Botticelli (*The Birth of Venus*), Dürer, Montaigne, La Fontaine, Renan, Maurras, Céline, or Montherlant, within a homogeneous Christian milieu, except that the risks of ending on the stake were very real before the

---

20 Pierre Manent, op. cit., p. 14.

18th century, as experienced by, among many others, the philosopher Giordano Bruno in Rome, in 1600.

When one evokes successive renaissances, that of the Carolingian epoch, then that of courtly love, and finally that of ancient rediscovery, one forgets that Christianity was itself profoundly composite, mixing sometimes conflictually Biblical heritage and that of Greek thought. We must be grateful to Pope Benedict XVI for having recalled this fundamental reality during his professorial lesson at the University of Regensburg, September 12, 2006: "The inner rapprochement between Biblical faith and Greek philosophical inquiry was an event of decisive importance not only from the standpoint of the history of religions, but also from that of world history — a fact that obliges us even today." One must pause for a moment on the heart of the reflection to be penetrated by it: "When one notes," says Benedict XVI, "this encounter, one can hardly be surprised that Christianity, despite its origin and its important development in the East, ended up finding in Europe a place of its decisive historical imprint."[21]

No one within the Church has proclaimed with such authority and force the anteriority of Greek heritage, nor the extent to which European Christianity had been transformed by Hellenic thought. One could add that the new religion was subsequently "barbarized," in the noble sense of the word, as we have said, by Germanic or Irish populations and the clerics of the early Middle Ages.

Century after century, awakenings are recorded by historians who wanted to take interest in them.[22] Their trace can already be detected at the time of the "Carolingian renaissance." Founded at the initiative of Alcuin, Charlemagne's advisor for intellectual and religious affairs, the Palatine Academy aimed to constitute a "new Athens" around the future emperor. It brought together scholars who chose a nickname.

---

21   I have extensively cited and commented on the lesson of Regensburg in *La Nouvelle Revue d'Histoire* no. 27, p. 15.

22   Guy Rachet, *Les Racines de notre Europe sont-elles chrétiennes et musulmanes?*, op. cit.

The poet Angilbert, abbot of Saint-Riquier, was Homer, which positioned him as the highest. For his part, Alcuin, abbot of Saint-Martin of Tours, called himself Horace, after the Latin poet and philosopher, a quite un-Christian singer of the tranquillity of soul and *carpe diem*.

For his part, Charlemagne had been kept apart from this spiritual filiation, which was reserved for an elite of scholars initiated into secret knowledge. His political power had not given him access to this knowledge. He therefore remained with the official teaching of the Church for whom there exists no history except for that entirely legendary one of the Old Testament. Charles (Karl) therefore chose as his pseudonym that of David, placed very high in the narrative of Scriptures but of little relation to the history of the Franks.

Ancient Presences in Medieval Literature

The return to sources anterior to Christianity is a constant among scholars. It is detectable under the mask of numerous hunted heresies, but also in popular festivals and medieval symbolism.[23] It is in literature that the awakening is most explicit, which has been well studied in the *Dictionary of French Letters: The Middle Ages*.[24] In his introduction to this vast panorama, Edmond Faral emphasizes a renewal of ancient Latinity starting in the year 800 and prepared by Irish masters: "There is in medieval literature a profane side that often relates it to the freest productions of literature in vernacular language [...] Excluded from official teaching, the doctrine of 12th-century philosophers who had returned to the study of profane Antiquity

---

23 See on this subject Nicole Belmont, *Paroles païennes, mythe et folklore* (Imago, 1986); Philippe Walter, *La Mythologie chrétienne. Fêtes, rites et mythes au Moyen Âge* (Imago, 2003); Michel Pastoureau, *Une histoire symbolique du Moyen Âge occidental* (Le Seuil, 2004).

24 *Dictionnaire des Lettres françaises. Le Moyen Âge* (Le Livre de Poche, "La Pochothèque," 1992).

had distant repercussions until the Renaissance…"[25] The clerics, who are partly laymen, will seek their inspiration in Virgil, Horace, Ovid, or Boethius.[26] In the quarrel that then puts admirers of the ancients against those who intend to reduce everything to commerce with Scriptures, it is the former who prevail.

"Never did the masters of Antiquity exercise domination comparable to that which was assured to them from Charlemagne to Saint Louis." Dissertations and debates parody sacred texts. By reaction, songs celebrate the invitations of spring, wine, love. The most turbulent of the clerics were the Goliards, a name given to rebellious scholars, vagabonds and undisciplined, present in the 12th–13th centuries in all the cities of France, England, and Germany. Beyond their erotic and Bacchic poems, they also bequeathed to us the fairy-like paganism of the *Carmina Burana*.

These Latin creations had their equivalent in "vernacular" language with *pastourelles* and *fabliaux*. Their comic stance and crudity expressed an astonishing freedom. In that time, it took audacity to tell the adventures of young Aucassin gaily renouncing paradise so as to go find all the joyous damned of this world in hell! The abundant profane iconography, less famous than religious iconography, testifies to a popular culture often refractory to the power of the Church.[27]

---

25 Having escaped Roman conquest and the forced Christianization that was its consequence after the 4th century, Ireland is the only Celtic territory where druid colleges were maintained. Rather than resist, they merged into the Church, starting with Saint Patrick in the 5th century, populating the monasteries of green Erin. We owe them a notable part of the transmission of ancient knowledge and letters before the 13th century. One may refer on this point to the study by Professor Christian J. Guyonvarc'h (University of Rennes) published in *La Nouvelle Revue d'Histoire* no. 21 (November 2005) (dossier devoted to the Celts and Gauls).

26 See Sylvain Gouguenheim, *Aristote au Mont-Saint-Michel* (Le Seuil, 2009); Guy Rachet, *Les Racines de notre Europe sont-elles chrétiennes et musulmanes?*, op. cit.

27 *Le Moyen Âge flamboyant. Poésie et peinture,* preface by Michel Zink (Paris, éditions Diane de Sellier, 2006).

During this same 12th century, at the court of Marie de Champagne, Chrétien de Troyes opened the cycle of Arthurian romances and courtly literature. This genre renewed Celtic imagination and an idea of love that one might have thought banished forever. The celebration of woman went against the misogynistic conception of the tempting and corrupting Eve. All this literature magnified the polarity of lady and knight, in harmony with chivalrous heroism. An ecclesiastical reaction was felt in the following century. But the success of pious novels and the principle of authority over free examination was provisional. From the 14th century, again, the irresistible love of life manifested itself.

A little more time passed before there came Montaigne, the most relevant of the French of the Renaissance. This gentleman of fresh age took pride in wanting to be of sword more than of robe. He was also a man who questioned himself in a world where the certainties of past centuries were toppling. He was the attentive spectator of three great ruptures that overturned the representations of his time: the discovery of the New World, of which the Scriptures had not breathed a word; the return of ancient thinkers, skeptical and tragic, who shook the Christian idea of Salvation; finally, the Reformation, which broke the unity of Christianity and generated the wars of religion. A foundation of prudence kept Montaigne from declaring himself too frankly. Yet, despite his protestations of fidelity to the Church, he referred more willingly to Homer or Seneca than to Jesus. He admired Emperor Julian and saluted Cato's suicide, professing a Stoic morality far removed from Christian humility and evangelical love. To tell the truth, he was more interested in living well and dying well than in "the other world." With Montaigne, we have yet another European making his return to the sources.

The Cult of the Virgin and Good Fairies

In his *France: An Adventure History*, Graham Robb, a good connoisseur of French literature and popular customs, devoted an interesting chapter to "Fairies, Virgins, Divinities and Priests," in other words: to the beliefs and "superstitions" of the countryside.[28]

He rightly insists on the permanences and similarities of practices throughout the former Gallic territory before 20th-century urbanization. Under Christianized appearances, "pagan" ancestral cults had survived everywhere. Miraculous stones and sacred springs continued to attract crowds, and good fairies survived under the traits of the Virgin. A famous example is that of the touching little Bernadette Soubirous, at Lourdes, in 1858. Her gentle visions of the Virgin in a Pyrenean grotto, accompanied by miraculous healings, attracted the superstitious faith of good people, while worrying the Church. The latter waited four years to grant its approval.

Twelve years earlier, in the diocese of Grenoble, on a mountain near the village of La Salette, the Virgin had also appeared to two little shepherds. There too, popular enthusiasm had forced the Church to homologate miraculous healings.

These strange phenomena were not exceptional. They fell in line with beliefs well anterior to Roman and Christian conquest. In popular vision, the Virgin, like good fairies, defended the poor, healed the sick, and avenged injustices. She was even attributed greater powers than God the father or his son Jesus, who were little invoked, except by theologians. For the clergy, the difficulty came from the fact that Bernadette's vision had occurred outside its intercession. It therefore inspired clerics with an anxiety that "betrayed a fear almost as old as the Church itself: that of no longer being indispensable."

---

28 Graham Robb, *Une Histoire buissonnière de la France* (Flammarion, 2011) [In English: Graham Robb, *France: An Adventure History* (New York: W. W. Norton, 2023)].

For centuries, supported by the political power associated with it, the Church had applied itself to razing or re-baptizing ancient pagan sites, often inventing new saints to supplant archaic divinities. Saint Anne, whose feet had never touched Armorica, was thus declared patron of Brittany. Her name indeed evoked that of the ancient Celtic goddess Ana who united this world to the beyond. She was therefore annexed. Names changed, but popular devotion to sacred sites was rarely abandoned.

These are some manifestations of how religiosity differs in accordance with peoples, cultures, and civilizations. It manifests itself among atheists as well as among believers. One notes it by observing the ecstasies provoked by the splendor and power of nature, or by the intoxicating harmony of music, not to mention the testimony, albeit sometimes debased, presented by the collective fervor aroused by spectacular sporting events.

The Pagan Temple of the Most Christian King

Since the rallying of bourgeois elites to political Catholicism between 1850 and 1950, particularly in France, it is difficult to get a somewhat precise idea of what the Christianization of Europe had been before the Counter-Reformation and the decisions of the Council of Trent. Catholic historian Jean Delumeau has nevertheless shown in his works that, until the 17th century, changes had remained quite superficial, most notably in the countryside, which remained attached to ancient superstitions and "pagan" practices under a Christian veneer.[29] As for elites, since the Renaissance and the rediscovery of the treasures of Antiquity, they practiced a strange syncretism mixing Christian devotion and the cults of ancient divinities.

One of the most revealing examples is that of the solar temple that is the château of Versailles, built by the imperious and attentive will of Louis XIV. Shortly after 1680, the château was almost completed, with

---

29   Jean Delumeau, *La Peur en Occident, XIVe-XVIIIe siècles* (Fayard, 1978).

its salons and the basins of its park exclusively dedicated to Greco-Roman divinities, Apollo, Diana, Latona, Ceres, Mars, Venus... This exclusive choice of the Apollonian world is surprising. Author of a remarkable study on Versailles, Yves Branca has shown that the château is "a terrestrial image of the palace of the Sun that Ovid describes in the fable of Phaethon, at the beginning of book II of the *Metamorphoses*."[30] There is nothing Biblical or Christian in this palace of the Most Christian king, protector of Molière to whom he had even suggested the character of Tartuffe...

Let us refer to Yves Branca's study: "The palace of Le Vau and the gardens it commands present a veritable sum of Greco-Roman wisdom [...] of which Louis XIV is an admirer in the person of Augustus, as he expresses very clearly in his *Memoirs* intended for the Dauphin. Solar symbolism will be affirmed there especially after the establishment of the Court [...] The mythological ornaments of the gardens and park are not arranged solely for the pleasure of whoever strolls through them. They recall the essential truths of ancient wisdom."

When, in 1675, out of the desire to temper the king's extramarital ardors, Bossuet entertained him "about the love of God and the ardent desire to follow his will," Louis responded with feigned ingenuity: "I have never heard talk of that, no one has told me anything about it."

Only the Affair of the Poisons, revealed in 1680, made Louis XIV descend from Olympus, marking a turning point in the reign and in the religious dispositions of the sovereign. We know that the principal favorite, the Marquise de Montespan, mother of seven royal bastards all legitimized, had been gravely compromised in this criminal affair of black magic. Though a good Christian according to the canons of the time, she had hoped to reconquer by magic the king's favors, despite a physique somewhat faded by age and successive pregnancies. The foundation of superstition that had led her to the extremities of black

---

30   Yves Branca, "Versailles, le palais du Soleil," a remarkable and knowledgeable study published in *La Nouvelle Revue d'Histoire* no. 57 (November–December 2011), p. 42 (dossier devoted to Louis XIV).

masses accompanied by sacrifices of newborns, would subsequently lead her to the most exalted bigotry, now in the hope of ensuring before her death her salvation in the beyond.

"The king believes himself devout," ironically observed Princess Palatine, Louis XIV's sister-in-law, a diarist without illusion of Versailles' escapades. In fact, each morning, in his sumptuous chapel, the king attended mass before going to hunt stag and ladies, never failing, moreover, in his overwhelming governmental functions. What did he do at mass? We know from the Palatine that he fingered his rosary, a restful occupation for the mind.

Antiquity knew the soothing benefits of prayer. Heroes frequently turned to the gods to implore them and request their support. As for simple mortals, they turned to heroes, notably Odysseus. He was a model, an archetype, that is to say a concentration of psychic energies. Archetypes are inspiring symbols. And what one says of Odysseus, one can say of his wife, Penelope. She was a helpful model, to whom any woman could think in torments or joys. Her pains, her waits, her stratagems, her final happiness, the support that Athena granted her, were sources of vigor. In Homer, behind each word hides an energy.

CHAPTER V

OUR FOUNDING POEMS

How do the Homeric poems concern us, we French and Europeans of the 21st century? The answer is self-evident. These poems are the foundation of European civilization, as well as of our literature and a significant part of our imagination. Within the same culture, human nature changes little, regardless of the magnitude of historical or social transformations. The fundamental questions remain the same: Who am I? What are we? Where are we going? To these questions, Homer has provided us with answers that remain valid, and he is the only one to do so with such depth. The more we are subjected to troubles caused by the incessant changes of technological domination, lifestyles, and philosophical and religious novelties, the more we need continuity and permanence — the more we need Homer.

The Educator of Ancient Greece and Europe

"The world is born, Homer sings! He is the bird of this dawn…" The visionary in Victor Hugo was not mistaken in associating Homer with the radiant dawn of our world.[1]

By Plato's own admission, Homer was the educator of ancient Greece, and therefore ours by way of spiritual inheritance and distant kinship. To Europeans who question themselves and their identity, the

---

1 Victor Hugo, *William Shakespeare*, Book II, chap. 2, § 1.

two great poems hold up a mirror in which to rediscover their true inner face, cleansed of what has disfigured them and often makes them wander, anxious and lost. Like Schliemann, the persistent discoverer of the site of Troy, if one digs beneath the strata accumulated by time, it is in the meditations of Homer that one rediscovers in vigorous freshness the soul of Europe, which merges with the spirit of the *Iliad*.

For Aristotle, who placed him at the summit of all literature, Homer was already the primary source of thought and life. In the 3rd century of our era, Plotinus and the Neoplatonists went so far as to deify Homer. They saw in him the direct contemplator of intelligible Beauty. At the beginning of *The Peloponnesian War*, Thucydides refers to the *Iliad* as an outline of the ancient history of the Greeks, thus recognizing Homer's merit in having laid the foundations of historical narrative. But this merit was little compared to all the others. Inspired by the gods and poetry, which are one and the same, Homer gave the Greeks and Europeans the founding books to which they could always refer in order to find themselves again.

Despite the succession of immense historical upheavals, the poet was still celebrated by the Palatine Academy under Charlemagne and during the Middle Ages. He was later celebrated by Dante in *The Divine Comedy* and by Petrarch, who had the poems translated into Latin. And Montaigne saw in Homer "the most perfect master in the knowledge of all things," which was repeated by Goethe, Nietzsche, Heidegger, Camus, Joyce and so many other contemporaries.

In 2007, the National Library of France (BNF) organized an exceptional exhibition entitled "Homer: In the Footsteps of Odysseus." The curators asked Jacqueline de Romilly to write a preface for their catalog. The great Hellenist concluded her remarks thus: "My master, Louis Bodin, a great specialist in Thucydides, told me shortly before his death: 'Now, for me, there is only Homer.' And it's a bit the same for me, now; one returns to the essential, to the absolutely pure."[2]

---

2   Jacqueline de Romilly devoted a magnificent book to the *Iliad* under the title *Hector* (Éditions de Fallois, 1997; Livre de Poche, 1999). By the same author,

With different words, this is also what the philosopher and Sinologist François Jullien says, known for his comparative work between European and Chinese thought: "When I was in *khâgne*," he confides, "my friend and I were called the Homerists — we read Homer in Greek like an open book... I have always had the feeling that there was something more crucial in these first lineaments of human thought than in the philosophy that was subsequently constructed and made explicit. And ever since I have been confronting these questions, I have become more and more convinced that, if one seeks the decisive categories of European thought ("the categories of action" as well as "the categories of knowledge"), it is in Homer that one must do so, well before Plato... Read [the *Iliad* and *Odyssey*] and you will obtain the decisive orientations of Greek philosophy."[3]

But Homer did not speak only for the Greeks. With a perfection of form not found elsewhere, he was the Greek expression of a conception of the world common to all Europeans, whether of Latin, Celtic, Slavic, or Germanic stock. This is what the work of Émile Benveniste and his disciple, Georges Dumézil, a great reader of Homer, has clearly shown. By comparing languages and myths, the two scholars have recognized the spiritual kinship of the Indo-Europeans, the common ancestors of the peoples of historical epochs.

The Transmission of the Founding Poems

Stunningly, while so many famous ancient works have disappeared, victims of sackings and centuries, Homer has triumphed over time and all disasters to reach us in entirety.

---

one can read in parallel her book of perfect concision, *Homère* ("Que sais-je?" collection, PUF, 1985).

3 François Jullien, interviews with Thierry Marchaisse, *Penser d'un dehors (la Chine). Entretiens d'Extrême-Occident* (Le Seuil, November 2000), p. 47.

Who was Homer? The contradictory hypotheses of modern scholars do not tell us.[4] Only what the Ancients thought matters, in my opinion. For them, the reality of the divine poet was never in doubt, even if various cities quarrelled to claim the privilege of being the place of his birth. The Ancients never doubted that he was the author of both the *Iliad* and the *Odyssey*. Around 430 before our era, Herodotus affirmed that Homer had lived four centuries before him, therefore in the 9th century. It is probably around this time that we can situate the invention of writing in Greece, based on an alphabet borrowed from the Phoenicians. Some specialists do not hesitate to associate the birth of writing and the transcription of oral epics.[5] They think that Homer, the genius poet of an earlier memory, could have been the inventor of a notation system that would have saved from oblivion the memory of the vanished heroes and his own composition. In truth, whether the poems were dictated or recomposed matters little, for the *Iliad* and *Odyssey* constitute the sacred legacy of our tradition, as shown by the rather miraculous character of their transmission.

In 2007, on the occasion of the great exhibition devoted to the origin and transmission of the poems, the BNF presented the rich collections of its Cabinet of Medals for the first time.[6] The commissioner of this exhibition, Patrick Morantin, emphasized that one "must first admire that at a distance of 3,000 years an ensemble of such magnitude has reached us. What veneration must have surrounded the work of the Poet, whatever the epochs, for this poetic mass to have traversed wars, vandalisms, accidents, censures, ignorance! How many works of late Antiquity have been lost while today we can read the *Iliad* and *Odyssey*

---

4   On the "Homeric question" (what we know of Homer), one can refer to Jacqueline de Romilly, *Homer* ("Que sais-je?", PUF, 1985), as well as Alexandre Farnoux, *Le prince des poètes* (Gallimard, 2010).

5   Alexandre Farnoux, op. cit., pp. 76–77.

6   The exhibition *Homère. Sur les traces d'Ulysse* ["Homer: In the Footsteps of Odysseus"] was accompanied by a rich catalog published by Seuil, realized by its three commissioners, Olivier Estiez, Mathilde Jamin and Patrick Morantin.

in their entirety!" Morantin added: "The *Iliad* is perhaps, with the New Testament, the work we know from the greatest number of sources."

In the 6th century before our era, three Athenian statesmen, Pisistratus and two of his sons, had established a written edition from earlier transcriptions. Later, between the 3rd-2nd centuries before our era, "Homer was the most studied author at the Museum of Alexandria [the principal center of Hellenistic study]; he was also the first subject of true edition. This critical activity begins with Zenodotus of Ephesus in the first half of the 3rd century before our era, and culminates with Aristarchus of Samothrace, in the first half of the following century [...] From the 2nd century before our era, the text becomes uniform. The work of the Alexandrian scholars had fixed a norm to which everyone henceforth referred."

The transmission of the poems suffered from the collapse of the Western Roman Empire, but without disappearing: "If, in the medieval West, the link with the original text of Homer was broken, the name of the Poet never ceased to be venerated and the memory of his heroes and their adventures was maintained. Homer continued indirectly to nourish the imagination of the Middle Ages through classical Latin poets like Virgil, Ovid, Statius, Latin summaries of the *Iliad*, apocryphal works by Dares the Phrygian and Dictys of Crete, medieval romances like the *Roman de Troie* [by Benoît de Sainte-Maure] and their prose adaptations [...] so that the heroes and the matter of the epic were known to the cultivated public when, by the Renaissance, the *Iliad* and the *Odyssey* were rediscovered in their original text."[7] During the Middle Ages, the kings of France, influenced by the *Aeneid*, which owed much to Homer, imagined themselves descended from an imaginary Trojan hero, named Francus or Francion, still invoked by

---

7   Catalog of the exhibition *Homère. Sur les traces d'Ulysse*, op. cit. This question has been studied by many scholars, notably Ernest Renan in his *Histoire de l'étude de la langue grecque dans l'Occident de l'Europe depuis la fin du ve siècle jusqu'à celle du xive*. This work, dating from 1848, retains its relevance. It was republished by Cerf in 2009.

Christine de Pizan in the 15th century. And the Germanic emperors thought themselves issued from the heroes of the *Iliad*.

After a momentary setting aside at the beginning of Christianization, the Byzantine Empire "watched over the transmission of ancient authors. The classical tradition was thus maintained in Byzantium, where, from 425 to 1453, the schools of Constantinople remained like its pillars. This is why it is improper to speak of 'renaissance' in the Eastern Roman Empire. In the West, on the other hand, the rediscovery of Homer was a significant fact for the first Italian humanists." At Petrarch's request, who did not read Greek, the first Latin translation of the *Iliad* was completed in 1366.

The defining event was the fall of Constantinople in 1453. Shortly before, many learned Byzantines had taken refuge in Italy. Thus appeared, in Florence in 1488, the first princeps edition in Greek of the *Iliad* and the *Odyssey*. In France, the first complete translation of the *Iliad* was completed in 1577 by the publisher Breyer. Much later, also renewing tradition, Empress Catherine II of Russia founded a port on the Black Sea in 1794. To affirm its European character facing Asia, she gave it the name of the Odessa, a Slavic translation of Odysseus.

A Sacred Epic

Composed around the 9th century before our era, thus 30 centuries ago, the *Iliad* and the *Odyssey* describe a civilization and heroes much more ancient still. These sacred poems tell us what we were in our dawn, like no others. Under the artifices of epic legend, they are rooted in a real history and in characters who, for the most part, existed. They give account of the distant and forgotten history of all other Europeans, Celts, Slavs, Germans or Scandinavians, whose great legends offer constant analogies with the representation of the world revealed by the *Iliad* and the *Odyssey*.

The two poems translate the originality of our being in the world, our way of being men and women in the face of life, death, childbirth, the city, destiny — in other words, the content and meaning of our existence. They place before us an ideal of life that has shaped our better part. By narrating the trials and passions of very distant ancestors through close kinship, they tell us that our anxieties, our hopes, our sorrows, and our joys have already been lived by our predecessors, who were also young, ardent sometimes to the point of madness, yet still wise and prudent. We are told of Achilles yielding to the impetuosity blood; Priam weeping over the death of his son; Helen the bewitched; Andromache, young wife and anxious young mother; Hector the valiant; Odysseus the cunning; Penelope, skillful and faithful; Nestor the wise; Telemachus the troubled adolescent... This proximity, despite the time elapsed, awakens the idea that we eternally pursue the same exceptional adventure in a world that is both beautiful and disturbing. The history of the heroes speaks to us of feelings and behaviors that are familiar to us, very different from those suggested by the most beautiful tales of Asia or the Orient. It speaks of respect for ancestors, communion with nature, stoic courage before the inevitable, attraction to what is noble and beautiful, contempt for baseness and ugliness. Full of pity for the often cruel fate of his heroes, Homer also expresses his admiration for them.

In the *Iliad*, the poet shows the lucid energy of men grappling with their destiny, devoid of illusion about the gods known for being subject to their whims, and hoping for no other resource than themselves and the strength of their soul. He shows them facing the mysterious powers of nature and their nature. Despite the omnipresence of divinities, the poet does not hold a religious or philosophical discourse. And yet, from his poem one can draw both a philosophy and a religiosity, as the Greeks did for as long as Hellas lived. Dostoevsky had understood this: "In the *Iliad*, Homer gave the ancient world an organization of spiritual life and terrestrial life just as strong as Christ gave to the new world."

Homer's Philosophical Legacy

Forming themselves through Homer's school, whose work embodied their spirit, the Greeks showed themselves to be great inventors
of myths with unlimited meanings. But they were little interested in
cosmogonic speculations. They preferred the finite to the infinite, the
measurable to the immeasurable. Their preferred hero was Odysseus,
who added to courage a logical and inventive spirit, manifested
among other things by the ruse of the Trojan horse (*Odyssey* VIII,
492–516). Was he not the protégé of Athena, the goddess whose philosophical symbol is the owl, the bird that sees in the darkness? The
Greeks' way of thinking pushed them to seek rational explanations
for phenomena, and to count only on themselves to understand the
universe. Attentive observation of the cosmos thus led them to distinguish visible phenomena from the invisible causes that govern them.

Thales of Miletus became the founder of mathematics by replacing
the empirical approach of the Egyptians and Babylonians with a true
science. In his *Descriptions of the Earth*, Hecataeus of Miletus became
the first geographer. Xenophanes of Colophon and Pythagoras of
Samos brought new materials to philosophical reflection by integrat-
ing geometry, arithmetic, and astronomy. Subsequently, Heraclitus of
Ephesus was the laconic theorist of the harmony of opposites and the
eternal return of life under changing forms. Later still, Democritus
illuminated the atomic structure of matter, Euclid confirmed the
foundations of geometry, while Aristarchus of Samos posited the
hypothesis that the Earth is a planet that revolves around its axis and
orbits the Sun. In a completely different register, Herodotus invented
historical inquiry based on facts, Hippocrates laid the foundations
of experimental medicine, Socrates and Plato imagined the infinite
possibilities of philosophical questioning, Aristotle fixed the rules of
logical thought, while Aeschylus and Sophocles transposed into their
theater the very spirit of tragedy. These epochs saw Praxiteles and

Phidias bring forth from marble the splendor of ideal human forms which one will not find at any other latitude.

These immense creations that Greek genius has bequeathed to us were contained in germ in the *Iliad* and the *Odyssey*. The two poems place the admiring observation of nature and the individuality of characters at the center of the narrative, to such an extent that one does not find in the tradition of any other civilization. None of the crushing divinities that are so frequent in the Orient or Asia imposes on them an arbitrary moral law under the threat of horrible punishments. In their very excesses, Homer's characters are never judged according to the abstract categories of an absolute moral good or evil, but rather according to what is noble, generous, equitable, or unworthy and base. The recognition of rooted individuality permeates the two poems. It was inscribed in statuary from the classical period. It irrigated political institutions, law, and the idea one forms of the freedom of the city, privilege of noble natures, and not the claims of helots.

By composing the *Iliad*, a narrative based on historical reality, as proven by the archaeological research of Heinrich Schliemann and his successors, Homer became the depository of the very ancient memory of the Achaean times that preceded him by several centuries. Subsequently, despite contrary influences, the spirit of the *Iliad* would never dry up. It was intimately associated with Memory, the Mnemosyne divinized by the Greeks. The poet, enlightened by the Muses, daughters of Memory, is the one who knows, remembers, and transmits.

For more than ten centuries, Homer was the educator of ancient Greece, much more than the philosophers who sometimes misunderstood him. He taught everything — courage as well as the *mêtis* so prized by Athena, in other words, practical intelligence, cunning, feints, stratagems, in which Odysseus was so prodigal for the better. Homer does not explain as the philosophers will; rather, he shows living examples, teaching the qualities that make a man an *agathos*, noble and accomplished. "Always be the best," says Peleus to his son Achilles, "prevail over all others" (*Iliad* VI, 208), a notion to which I will return. To be beautiful and brave for a man, gentle, loving, and faithful for a woman, which excludes neither audacity nor valor. The poet has bequeathed in condensed form what ancient Greece subsequently offered to posterity: respect for sacred nature, excellence as a life ideal, beauty as horizon.

A Reading of Homer

I propose here my own reading of Homer, by no means that of a scholar or a Hellenist. It is the reading of a lover of the text, of a historian who savors and compares it, of a European who meditates on it by according it a current scope. Summarizing the two poems in broad strokes, I will emphasize what they contain of the timeless. Stripping the heroes of their helmet and breastplate, I do not perceive them "in costume" of a dated epoch, but as archetypes outside of time and therefore always current. I wish to show that Homer is not reserved for a minority of scholars. He belongs to the fervor of all his readers.

At the moment of my writing, most Europeans have given up reading and learning by heart the text in ancient Greek, as was once done in high school. But they will find without difficulty in their library, at an old uncle's, in the paperback section or even sometimes on the "Web," a variety of translations giving them access to the magic of the text. Granting themselves a few hours of pleasure, isolating themselves from daily noise, forgetting school exercises, the modern reader can immerse himself in these old masterpieces, which are always young.

The prodigiously inventive style of the poems seems at first disconcerting, especially with its attributions of numerous repetitions that served as landmarks for the listeners of Antiquity who heard them and did not read them. But one must enter the text, read it half-aloud, and one is soon enchanted.

In composing the *Iliad*, Homer became the creator of the first tragic epic and, with the *Odyssey*, that of the first novel. He does not conceptualize as the philosophers will do, but rather he gives to see, bequeathing to posterity a life ideal and a poetization that, from the worst misfortune, can bring forth this light of the senses that we call "beauty" and which arouses this admiring shiver.

In the *Iliad* especially, one is stunned by the exuberance of comparisons with natural elements and phenomena — rivers, winds, storms, snow showers, fires… — but also with animals — wolves, boars, horses… — or again by the abundance of countryside life scenes with the rhythm of daily work. And what inventiveness! Speaking of the beauty of Diomedes, transfigured by Athena, the poet writes: "One would have said the star of late summer, all brilliant with its greatest splendor, after its bath in the Ocean." Homer delights in magnifying everything, the humblest gestures like those of warriors. He indulges in a sort of incessant recall of a universe where the stars shine, where flights of birds cross skies charged with storm, where men work the earth and hunt game through fields where one glimpses a donkey getting drunk on ripe grain… The tasks of each day — the preparation of meals, the cutting and cooking of meats, the maintenance of fire in the hearth… — and the familiar environment — the utensils of the house, the goblets where wine flows… — are all described with relish and admiration. The everyday is transformed before our eyes. Light and night are divine. The storm at sea is the anger of a god. The poet feels life as a permanent miracle. Under his amazed gaze, the gods take form, to the point that even the wasp nests at the edge of paths seem to be divinized, and the spectacle of a beautiful naked body is enveloped in the voluptuous effluvia of a perfume.

A long time ago, one Christmas Eve, finding myself in a bookstore of old books in Paris, I discovered an original bound edition of the *Iliad* and the *Odyssey* in the translation published by Leconte de Lisle in 1856.

I had been looking for this edition for a long time, keeping the memory of my first enchanted readings, long ago, in a volume from my father's library. Escaping from the city as quickly as possible to savor my prey in my lair, I began to reread the first stanzas of the *Iliad* half-aloud so that its music would resound, which one must always do. The archaic and rough form adopted by Leconte de Lisle for proper names (Akhilleus for Achilles) accentuates the vigor of the incantation on which the poem opens:

"Sing, Goddess, of Peleus' son Akhilleus' fatal anger, which brought infinite woes to the Akhaians [Achaeans], and sent to Aides [Hades] so many strong souls of heroes, themselves delivered as prey to dogs and birds of prey. And Zeus' design was accomplished [...]"

In pencil, I corrected the translation, replacing "disastrous anger" with "fatal anger," and "carnivorous birds" with "birds of prey," which sounded better to my ears.

Translated with harshness by Leconte de Lisle, despite some unfortunate omissions, the poem regains its mysterious force as a sacred text that the six university translations in my possession do not always have the power to restore. The author of *Barbarous Poems* was an inspired one. His successors were often no more than good scholars. Albeit with some exceptions, did they understand anything about the universe of blood, passion, love, and beauty that is Homer's?[8]

The Greek Expression
of the Hyperborean Heritage

From these poems, we are born, and yet the first is that of war, which is indeed troubling...

---

8   Among these notable exceptions: the works of Jacqueline de Romilly; Marcel Conche, *Essais sur Homère* (PUF, 1999); Alexandre Farnoux, *Homère* (Gallimard, 2010); to which I would add the fervent essay by Georges Haldas, *Ulysse et la lumière grecque* (L'Âge d'Homme, 1998), which a friend introduced me to.

The *Iliad*, this poem of war, is also one of love. But not everything is yet said. Intimately linked to the *Odyssey*, the *Iliad* is above all the poem of life and death, the two poles of our destiny. I do not believe that any other work that has sprung from the genius of men or gods, under any other latitude, responds like the *Iliad* and the *Odyssey* to the questions posed by the European spirit. This is why they were the sacred poems of the ancient Greeks, educating them in everything. They are therefore also ours by inheritance. They respond to the immense trouble into which our epoch has thrown us and which spares nothing — politics, religion, education, work, family. and the very idea one forms of oneself.

While they were no longer supported by any power, any Church, any institution, and while so many other magnificent works have disappeared, Homer's poems have reached us, intact, crossing centuries and upheavals, never ceasing to fascinate and stimulate great and small minds, generation after generation. If we read them with a fresh gaze, stripped of the erudition of the learned, these poems of love, adventure and war continue to speak to us even today.[9] Whence, then, this permanence, when our societies have gone from being martial to mercantile and our cities, once peopled with heroes, are now of simple men?

These sacred poems are the Greek expression of a heritage common to all our European or Borean ancestors, whether Celtic, Germanic, Slavic, or Latin.

I have just used the neologism *Borean*, which requires an explanation. I use it to avoid equivocations about the word "European,"

---

9   The translations of the poems are numerous in modern French. Apart from what I have said about Leconte de Lisle's translation, my preferences for the *Iliad* go to Paul Mazon's translation (Les Belles Lettres, 1938; Gallimard, "Folio Classique" collection, wherein Vidal-Naquet's preface adds nothing). For the *Odyssey*, I stick to Philippe Jaccottet's translation (La Découverte, 1982; "Poche" collection, 2004). One can also refer to the volume Homère, *l'Iliade, l'Odyssée*, translated by Robert Laffont ("Bouquins" collection, 1995), whose critical apparatus is of interest.

sometimes put to dubious uses. "Boreans" designates Europeans of ancient stock.

This term has a broader meaning than "Indo-Europeans," which is used mainly in linguistics. It proceeds from the Greek myth of origins reported by Herodotus, Plutarch, and Diodorus of Sicily. For the Greeks, the mythical people of the Hyperboreans (those who live beyond the breath of Boreas, the North Wind) lived a blessed existence in the North. They are sometimes confused with the Celts. The Hyperboreans were worshippers of Apollo, who, according to legend, spent the three months of winter with them. Offerings attributed to this original people arrived each year at Apollo's sanctuary in Delos, after having wandered from city to city.

"We Hyperboreans," writes Nietzsche at the beginning of fragment 167 of *The Will to Power*. The memory had thus been transmitted! "We Hyperboreans…"

Trojans and Achaeans

In 16,000 verses and 24 cantos, the *Iliad* reports a brief episode of 51 days at the end of the 10 years of the siege of Troy, probably in the 13th century before our era. As Heidegger noted, this poem is voluntarily bounded, just like the *Odyssey*. But, within the limits of a single episode of the Trojan War, it reveals an entire interpretation of the world and life.

Troy, otherwise called Ilion (hence the "*Iliad*"), is a powerful fortified city, built at the entrance to the Dardanelles, on the Asian coast of the Hellespont, a constant frontier between the West and the East. No more than today's historians, those of Antiquity, including Herodotus and Thucydides, doubted the reality of the events that served as the framework for the *Iliad*. The Trojans were Boreans of the same race as their Greek adversaries, the "fair-haired" Achaeans. With the difference that the Trojans were associated with Asia, and not only for geographical reasons. Their city is governed by a patriarchal order and not by that of the feudal freedom of the Achaeans which prefigured the order of the Greek city.[10] The Trojan army includes barbarian contingents. It is not governed by the strict order of the Achaean army. Homer compares it to grasshoppers, while that of the Achaeans evokes for him the order of a swarm of bees.

In a famous passage of the *Iliad* (XIII, 130–131, Mazon translation), the poet describes the Achaean phalanx: "Lance makes a rampart for lance, shield for shield, each supporting the other; shield leans on shield, helmet on helmet, warrior on warrior." What one glimpses here is not merely the prefiguration of the political order, but above all the expression of what is a solidary community, where each member can rely on the others, where the desertion of a single one would instantly annihilate the indissociable whole. There is no question of "contract" here, but instead of mutual obligations inscribed in the founding pact of clan, tribe, city, and phalanx.

According to tradition, the conflict was of mythical origin, involving the gods who were split between the two camps.[11] Aphrodite had granted to the Trojan Paris, one of the sons of old King Priam, the power to seize Helen, the most beautiful of women, already married to the "fair-haired" Menelaus, an Achaean, the King of Sparta. The rape of a royal wife by a foreigner was a crime that struck all the Achaeans. At the wedding, each of the Greek lords had sworn to ensure respect for the union of Menelaus and the all too desirable Helen. After the rape, an army assembled at Aulis with its swift ships and headed for

---

10   Pierre Manent has devoted a long reflection to the origins of the Greek city in the Homeric poems in *Les Métamorphoses de la cité. Essai sur la dynamique de l'Occident* (Flammarion, 2010), pp. 40–80.

11   Homer does not report the origins of the legend that all Greeks knew. At the wedding of Peleus (Achilles' father) and the nymph Thetis, Eris (Discord) threw a golden apple (the "Apple of Discord") bearing the inscription "for the most beautiful." The goddesses Hera, Athena, and Aphrodite wanted to seize it and referred to Paris to settle the dispute, each making him an extraordinary promise. Paris granted the apple to Aphrodite and received from her in reward the possession of Helen.

the Asian shores of the Troad. Troy will be avenged and Helen brought back. Thus begins the war: "All the earth, in the distance, laughed with the gleam of bronze…"

Achilles' Fatal Anger

After ten years of a very long siege, accompanied by raids all around, a quarrel pits Agamemnon, leader of the Achaean coalition, against Achilles, the most famous hero of his camp, a young and quite immature colossus. Abusing his power, Agamemnon seizes Briseis "of beautiful cheeks," the young captive beloved by Achilles. Such is the pretext and the beginning of the poem: "Sing, goddess, of Achilles' fatal anger […]" — this goddess who sings the epic is the Muse of memory, of which the poet is the interpreter, which underscores his link with the divine world. Thus begins the *Iliad*.

In the grip of just anger, after having copiously insulted Agamemnon, Achilles implores his mother, Thetis, to avenge him by imploring that Zeus[12] make success elude the Achaeans when Achilles decides to abandon the battle. He "withdraws to his tent" (the formula will become established) along with his men, the Myrmidons (canto I). And so it shall be. Zeus' will shall be fulfilled to the detriment of the Achaeans. One can enter into the game of this divine intervention or see in it the mythical transposition of natural chains of events.

Whatever the case, the anger of Achilles, the principal hero of the *Iliad* alongside the Trojan Hector, is the pivot of the poem. His and his men's withdrawal from combat has the most serious consequences for the Achaeans. Victory abandons them. On the plain under the walls of

---

12　Homer's world is divided into three categories of actors that relate less to theology than to poetry. At the very top are the Olympian gods, reigned over by Zeus. They are in no way the creators of the world and life, but are part of it at a superior rank. They have exceptional powers that merge with the powers of Nature. Above all, they are immortal. They have received the power to mate with mortals of both sexes to give birth to heroes, who are of a superior essence to that of simple humans, but, unlike the gods, are not immortal.

Troy, they will suffer three increasingly disastrous defeats. From being the assailants, they are reduced to the defensive. They must even build an entrenched camp around their ships. This entrenchment is soon forced by the Trojans led by Hector, the most famous son of Priam. The enemy is about to set fire to the Greeks' ships and throw them into the sea.

Throughout these hard battles that fill the poem with carnage and exploits, Achilles' absence is nothing other than the striking sign of his indispensable force. The bravest of the Achaean chiefs, the massive Ajax, the impetuous Diomedes, and the skillful Odysseus all try in vain to replace him.

The Kinship of Men and Natural Forces

One night of black tragedy, between two disasters, withdrawn under his tent, Achilles is gnawing at himself in the inactivity to which he has condemned himself. Suddenly, he sees an incoming delegation led by the two greatest chiefs of the army, Ajax and Odysseus. The old Phoenix has joined them and tries to make him hear the voice of reason. Facing danger, Agamemnon has repented. He returns Briseis (whom he has not touched) and offers sumptuous gifts as reparation. As is fitting, one begins with libations. Then one comes to the point. Ajax, Odysseus, and Phoenix speak in turn to convince Achilles to renounce his vengeance. They speak of Agamemnon's repentance, de-scribe the gifts offered by him to obtain his pardon and reconciliation. Nothing works. The mission fails. Achilles persists and perseveres in his rancor, putting himself at fault in turn (canto IX).

The next day, the Trojans force through the Greeks' defenses, threatening to throw them into the sea. Hector already sets a ship on fire. At the other end of the camp, Achilles sees the flames rise. Despite his obstinacy, he cannot remain insensitive to the supplications of Patroclus, another of himself.[13] He agrees to send his troops back into battle and clothes Patroclus in his own armor. This counter-offensive drives back the Trojans. However, after hard combat, Patroclus is killed by Hector (canto XVI). Achilles' pain is so intense that it brings him back to life, unleashing in him a vengeful fury against Hector.

Thus, the poem operatively proceeds through a complete reversal of the dramatic action that had been frozen by Achilles' withdrawal. Mad with grief, the Achaean hero returns to combat: "Like a prodigious fire rages through the deep valleys of a dried mountain, the forest burns, and the wind, which pushes it in all directions, makes the flame whirl. So in all directions bounds Achilles. He went, like the night…" (canto XVIII). This is a constant in Homer: to compare men to the forces of nature, and certainly not for simple literary artifices. This constant highlights their intimate kinship.

Achilles' Reversal

After several vicissitudes and a fierce duel, Achilles kills Hector (canto XXII), then he pays homage to Patroclus' remains, organizing funeral games in his honor (canto XXIII), sacrificing several young Trojan prisoners on his friend's funeral pyre. Achilles then gives himself over to his still unsatisfied rage for vengeance, raging against Hector's corpse, dragging it endlessly in the dust behind his chariot (canto XXIV).

However, the last canto of the *Iliad* is also the theater of Achilles' reversal, prisoner until then of his excess. Homer suggests that his excess

---

13 Patroclus was Achilles' cousin; he was his childhood companion. Being a little older, Achilles played the role of his elder brother, which explains the deep attachment that unites the two men. A parallel is to be noted between Achilles and Lancelot of the Lake, the hero (much later) of Arthurian legends: the first has a nymph for mother, the second, although son of mortals, was raised by a fairy, Viviane — the Lady of the Lake — who will make him an accomplished knight before leading him to King Arthur's court.

has ended up wearying the best-disposed gods. We will therefore see Achilles pass from vengeful fury to compassion when Priam comes to implore him to return his son's body. Guided by the gods, the old king takes Achilles' knees and kisses his terrible hands that have killed so many of his sons: "Remember your own father, Achilles, equal to the gods. Your father is like me at the cursed threshold of old age, with perhaps no one to ward off misfortune and ruin from him. But he at least has the happiness, in his heart, to know you are still alive, and he can hope to see you return from Troy. But me, my misfortune is infinite. I gave birth to sons, all brave, but none of them remains to me. The only one who still remained to protect our city, yesterday you killed him. It was Hector! And it is for him that I am here, to buy him back with an immense ransom. Respect the gods, Achilles, and take pity on me, in memory of your father. I have endured what no mortal has yet endured. I have kissed the hand of the man who killed my son…" (*Iliad* XXIV, 486–506).

This astonishing scene sees the old king humble himself out of love for his son. And the terrible Achilles, suddenly moved, will show himself accessible to pity. He returns Hector's remains to Priam, weeping with him over the fate of young warriors sacrificed. Transformed by his own suffering, the hero suddenly reveals himself to be more complex than his savage violence suggested.

Achilles Knows His Destiny and Has Chosen It

Along with Hector the Trojan, Achilles is the hero who dominates the *Iliad* at a great height from the very first stanza. His pain over the death of Patroclus that unleashed his fury is compounded by the prescience of his own fate. As he recalled to Odysseus and the ambassadors of canto IX, an ancient prediction holds that he will be killed as soon as he has taken Hector's life. This he knows. Unlike other heroes, he knows his destiny in advance and has chosen it. Very young, the choice was offered to him between a long and peaceful life

far from battle, or an intense and brief life, cut short in battle. And it
is the latter that he wanted. However, free of illusions, he knows that
he will have no other life: "The life of a man," he says in canto IX,
"is not found again; never again does it let itself be taken or seized,
from the day it has left the enclosure of his teeth..." This is a thought
that speaks to us just as it spoke to the ancient Greeks, who, it is said,
made canto IX their favorite.

Let us insist for a moment on what the choices of Achilles, Hector,
Helen, Penelope, and Odysseus suggest. In Homer, life, this small,
ephemeral, so common thing, has no value in itself. It is only worth its
intensity, its beauty, the breath of greatness that each man — and first
in his own eyes — can give it. This is a very different conception from
that conveyed by so many bazaar wisdoms, the platitudes that have
invaded the spirit of the Western masses and incited the desire to live
a life as long as possible, even if mediocre and larval.

Mortal like all beings of nature, plant or animal, men are, however,
sometimes splendid like the immortal gods. Homer shows them often
even greater, because they are mortal.

The Freedom of Homer's Heroes

Compared to what the sacred texts of other peoples and other cultures show, the freedom and sovereignty of Homer's heroes is unique.
Certainly, the gods intervene in the *Iliad*, in season and out of season,
but without really weighing on the autonomy of men. Their numerous interventions only precipitate what would have been accomplished anyway. And one clearly feels that Homer does not take them
quite seriously (except perhaps Athena), which scandalized Plato, a
great spirit no doubt, but stiff and moralizing.

In reality, Homer's gods, unlike the crushing and even monstrous
gods of other religions, are most often transpositions of the forces of
nature and life. These very human gods (except for their privilege of
immortality) are also pretexts that Homer uses to broaden his palette

of psychological situations. Thus, we see Hera use all the artifices of erotic seduction (not forgetting perfumes) to circumvent Zeus, her divine spouse (*Iliad* XIV). Then this same Zeus, awakened after love, and furious at having been deceived, vigorously scolds his wife during a domestic scene that would not surprise in a boulevard comedy (canto XV). But these are only brief recreations in the vast symphony of the tragic epic. The gods regain their function as symbols of an order of things that always reminds humans of itself. Thus, in canto IV, when the poet suggests the awakening of aggressiveness and hatred through the intervention of a divinity called Discord: "Ares animated the Trojans, and Athena, the goddess with gray eyes, breathed through the ranks Fear, Panic and Discord […] who, small at first, suddenly rises, and her head rises to the sky, while her feet trample the earth" (IV, 439–443). This is indeed how we know Discord ("furious and excessive"). The metaphor of divine intervention reveals the passions and rages buried in the depths of us, "head raised to the sky and feet trampling the earth."

Helen: The Gods are Guilty of Everything

There are not only gods, heroes, and warriors in the *Iliad*, there are also women (Helen, Briseis, Hecuba, and Andromache), children (Astyanax), and old men (Priam and Nestor). There are also not only brave ones. There is, for example, Thersites, who is at once cowardly, ugly, and lame, also speaking without measure "like a jackdaw," intervening inappropriately in the council to contest royal authority, which earns him a beating from Odysseus (*Iliad* II). There is Paris, whose strange lovemaking with Helen is at the origins of the war. Executing Aphrodite's will, he was the seducer and ravisher of Helen. Involuntary initiator of the conflict, it is he who will also end it by killing Achilles with a treacherous arrow, before he himself is killed — episodes which the poem does not report, that only the prophecy formulated by Hector at the moment of his death suggests (XXII, 359–360).

Paris, the often cowardly and vain pretty boy, is at the antipodes of his brother Hector, who despises him. Hector is the pure hero, the protector of Troy, while Paris is the "scourge of his homeland." The woman he has abducted and seduced despises him just as much and does not hesitate to tell him so: "So there you are back from combat! Ah! You would have done better to perish there under the blows of the powerful warrior who was my first husband!" (III, 428–436). She detests him, but, by Aphrodite's will, she is enslaved to his sexual magnetism. Once again, Homer does not explain, he tells. And what he says is full of complex human truth.

Helen is the opposite of Paris. She is moral in the face of her amoral lover. She revolts against the physical submission that Aphrodite and her sexuality impose on her. Her nature was made for order. She never ceases to regret the time when everything was arranged in her life: "I left my nuptial chamber, my relatives, my dear daughter... So I languish in tears." Nothing predisposed her to play the role of the adulterous woman, instrument of the ruin of two peoples. Nothing, except the intervention of the gods, which has so much importance in the life of men and women precisely where sexual attraction is concerned, which is something other than love.

Far from being models of perfection, Homer's heroes are subject to error and excess in proportion to their very vitality. They pay the price for it, but they are never subjected to transcendental justice punishing sins as defined by a God external to them. Neither the pleasure of the senses, nor that of force, nor the games of sexuality are assimilated to evil. Only excess is shown as a fault that can endanger the order of life.

The current interpretation has too much neglected the profound significance of an essential moment of canto III of the *Iliad* (III, 161–175), which responds in advance to the frightening weight that other religions will make humans bear with the idea of the Fall and Fault. It is the moment when the old King Priam invites the too beautiful Helen onto the walls of Troy to describe to him the two armies present, while a truce has just been concluded. Well aware of being the involuntary cause of the war, Helen laments, saying she would rather be dead. Priam then responds with infinite gentleness that surprises us: "No, my daughter, you are guilty of nothing. It is the gods who are guilty of everything!" This is such delicacy and a stunning height of view on the part of the old king, all of whose sons will be killed. And on Homer's part, what generous and superior wisdom, which frees humans from the imaginary guilt with which other beliefs will burden them.

By placing these words in Priam's mouth, Homer does not say that men are never guilty of the misfortunes that strike them. He shows elsewhere how much vanity, envy, anger, stupidity and other flaws can provoke calamities. But in the specific case of this war, as in many wars, he emphasizes that the essential escapes human will. It is the gods, fate, or destiny that decide.

Centuries of known history have taught us how sensible this interpretation is. How can one not be struck by its wisdom when so many religions accuse humans and their supposed sins of all the disasters of which they are victims, including earthquakes?[14]

But Priam's words have an even broader scope. They suggest that, in human life, many faults are often the effect of fate. This distance in relation to the mysteries of existence and this respect for others is a constant in the poems. One can see in it proof of the high level of civility and wisdom of the world that Homer describes, to such an extent that, by comparison, ours could often appear barbarous.

---

14 The Church interpreted the terrible tsunami that destroyed Lisbon in 1755 as celestial punishment akin to that which, according to the Bible, was reserved for Sodom and Gomorrah, which were destroyed because of the immorality of their inhabitants. Voltaire ironized: were the newborns killed in the cataclysm also guilty of the vices attributed to their parents?

Hector's Stoicism and Patriotism

Achilles is the incarnation of youth. He is also the incarnation of force. He is the radiant and untamed force before which everything bows. A force subject to passion. Achilles dominates nothing, he suffers everything. This is clearly seen with Briseis, Agamemnon, Patroclus, and Hector. Circumstances unleash within him one tempest after another. Everything in him defies death. He thinks little of it, though he knows it is near. He loves life enough to prefer its intensity to its duration. His love of glory, his impatience and his anger keep him away from action during the first eighteen cantos of the poem, to the point of endangering his own people. To save the army, it would suffice for him to rise, as Odysseus tells him: "Rise and save the army..."

We have all known, closely or distantly, in private relations or in public life, exceptional characters of unpredictable temperament, prey to their ardor, their pride, capable of unleashing catastrophes or provoking saving impulses.

Awakened by Patroclus' death, Achilles rises, the incarnation of force: "Achilles rose... A high clarity radiated from his head to the sky, and he advanced to the edge of the ditch. There, standing, he uttered a cry, and this voice aroused among the Trojans an unspeakable tumult" (XVIII).

Everything opposes him to Hector, to whom Homer's sympathy implicitly goes. The poem of the Achaeans presents their principal enemy as an example. This is yet another manifestation of the sacred book's nobility. If he is as brave as Achilles, Hector is not carried by blind bravery. He incarnates the very figure of tragic courage. He does not ignore fear. He must make an effort to overcome it. He even has a moment of yielding to panic and fleeing from Achilles before recovering (canto XXII). Sensing that his fate is sealed, he will fight to the end of his strength.

Hector is also the incarnation of patriotism. For him, honor merges with duty. He is ready to die, not for his own glory, but for his kingdom, his wife and his child. He will defend them against all hope, for he senses that Troy is lost.

There is nothing more carnal and more relevant than Hector's love for his homeland, of which his wife and son are the concrete images. He does not hide his anxieties from Andromache before leaving her to return to combat: "I know that a day will come when sacred Troy will perish, and Priam, and Priam's people. But neither the future misfortune of the Trojans, nor that of my mother, of King Priam and my brave brothers, afflicts me as much as yours, when a bronze-armored Achaean will ravish your freedom and take you away weeping… May the heavy earth cover me dead before I hear your cries, before I see you torn from here…" (VI, 447–465). Having confessed this despair, he extends his arms toward his son. But the child bursts into sobs, terrified by his father's gleaming helmet. This makes Hector laugh. He removes his helmet and entrusts the child to Andromache, who takes her son in her arms "with a laugh in tears." An astonishing moment where Homer's poetic genius bursts forth.

This "laugh in tears" is, however, much more than a simple literary find. It is the condensed essence of many dramatic situations of existence, when pain and a comic image allowing one to bear it are mixed.

Hector recovers. With delicacy, he corrects his dark predictions: "Cease to be afflicted," he tells Andromache, "No one can send me underground before the fixed hour…"

The moment before, Andromache was begging Hector not to expose himself. Now, she calms down. She feels that he defends her freedom and their mutual tenderness. There is in this last conversation of the two spouses something unique in ancient literature.

The poem ends much later with the preparation of Hector's funeral, without the episodes of Achilles' death or the "Trojan horse" which will be briefly evoked in the *Odyssey* (cantos XI and VIII).[15]

The *Odyssey*: Harmony with the Cosmic Order

The second of the great poems tells in 12,000 verses and 24 cantos of Odysseus' difficult return to his homeland — a return hindered by a thousand formidable traps.

The *Odyssey*, thus, is the poem of return, of *nostos*, the word which yielded "nostalgia" and by which the Greeks expressed their intense desire for native land. It is also the poem of just vengeance.

But the *Odyssey* is more than that. Under narrative pretexts which are different from the *Iliad*, the second poem suggests the "worldview" proper to the Hellenes. It shows man's place in nature and his relationship with the mysterious forces that command it.

The harmonizing of mortals with the cosmic order is at the heart of the Homeric poems. But Homer's Heaven is placed beyond the primitive epochs of the foundation of the cosmos evoked by myths and legends even more ancient, whose content will be shaped in Hesiod's *Theogony*: the confrontation of Uranus and Cronos, the battle of the gods and their victory over the Titans. Here, the chthonic part is forgotten. The poet retains only the Olympian light, that of the Hyperborean conquerors of Hellas. With an audacity inconceivable

---

15 According to a legend that the *Iliad* does not report, Zeus would have decided on the destruction of Troy and Priam's race, who were guilty in his eyes of having begotten Paris and favored Helen's rape. Conversely, he would have wanted to spare a lateral branch, that of Aeneas, son of Aphrodite and Anchises, descendant of the founder Dardanus, like Priam himself. Aeneas was Troy's most valiant defender after his cousin Hector, and Zeus promised him a high destiny after the destruction of the city, which he could flee while carrying his father on his shoulders. Much later, in the *Aeneid*, Virgil gathered the ancient legends to make Aeneas the future founder of Rome, the new Troy of Latium. Virgil connected Augustus' family to that of Aeneas.

in the religions of the Orient, he elevates Greek man to the image of the gods and becomes the latter's sometimes irreverent or ironic interpreter. According to Goethe's word, "Greek religion did not make divinity human: it saw the essence of man as divine." Allowing men to connect to their divine part and to cosmic forces will be the goal of Greek wisdom.

Such is also the significance of the rupture and then the reconquest of the cosmic order that serves as the framework for the *Odyssey*. Involuntarily, Odysseus has provoked the anger of Poseidon by blinding his son, the cyclops Polyphemus. Such is the destiny of men. Without having wanted it, they provoke disasters and the anger of the gods. Then, they must fight and endure torments to rediscover the lost harmony. Such will be Odysseus' fate. Confronting the terrifying ordeals imposed by Poseidon, who has plunged him into the world of chaos, that of monsters (Charybdis and Scylla) and possessive or perverse creatures (Circe, Calypso, the Sirens), the navigator tirelessly battles to escape traps and rediscover his place in the cosmic order. From traps to mortal perils, it will take him ten years to return home. This is no mere pretext for Homer to charm his public with fantastic stories. Odysseus' long journey is driven by the invincible desire to escape chaos and rediscover the ordered cosmos of "bread-eating" men. No doubt, love for Penelope and nostalgia for Ithaca have a strong place in this desire for return. But they only translate the hope of being once again fitted within the order of the world, in order to rediscover and reconquer his homeland. Thus will he regain footing in the order of generations, like a fragment of eternity.

Telemachus: The Recourse to Time

The novel of Odysseus and Penelope, the *Odyssey* is also that of Telemachus, their son. Born just after Odysseus' departure for the conquest of Troy, he is absent from the *Iliad*, whereas he is the principal hero of the first four cantos of the *Odyssey*. We find him again in the final phase of the adventure, from canto XV on, where he will act in his father's shadow to reconquer Ithaca and eliminate the "suitors." This strong presence makes part of the poem a Telemachy (the battle of Telemachus).

To escape the plot of the "suitors" who have come to occupy the palace of Ithaca and lay siege to Penelope, the adolescent, watched over and guided by Mentor-Athena, sets sail to search for his father. He lands at Pylos and meets Nestor, who has returned from Troy and who encourages him to avenge his mother and rid himself of the "suitors." He then stays at Sparta, where Helen has resumed her place beside Menelaus.

While Odysseus' son, comforted, prepares to return to Ithaca, the "suitors" devise a trap to kill him. He will elude it thanks to Athena's help. This sometimes dangerous journey weaves the framework of a true *Bildungsroman*, which Abbé Fénelon wanted to exploit for the composition of his famous 1699 novel intended for the Dauphin's edification.[16]

Since the first canto of the *Odyssey*, we have seen the young man, at first an indecisive adolescent, evolve. Little by little, he asserts himself to the point of speaking harshly to his mother. Then he takes the initiative of an assembly of Ithaca's citizens to have his rights respected in the face of the "suitors." The aggressiveness of the latter and his total solitude then put him in a desperate situation.

Athena's intervention will doubly save him from disaster. Not only does she organize his escape and his sea voyage to Pylos and Sparta, arranging comforting encounters with Nestor, Helen, and Menelaus, but she also makes time play in his favor. Athena's interventions can be interpreted as allegories of the practical intelligence she embodies.

This is neither the first nor the last time that Homer suggests the importance of time and strategic withdrawals to resolve a hopeless situation. In the *Iliad*, by withdrawing to his tent after Agamemnon's

---

16   *The Adventures of Telemachus.*

initial affront, Achilles let events run and ripen without intervening, until the moment of his thunderous return to battle. Odysseus will act similarly several times in the *Odyssey*, notably in the final phase of Ithaca's reconquest ("Patience, my heart!"). Thus, in poems where heroes are constantly required for action, an attentive gaze allows one to distinguish, at the very heart of the strategies they elaborate, long spaces of time where they withdraw while waiting for a propitious moment to act, which sometimes takes a long time. This thoughtful attitude is characteristic of Odysseus, whose skill and cunning Homer constantly praises. Odysseus is a man of action, certainly, but one who knows how to grant "time to time" and wait for the course of things to turn in his favor. The value of this teaching is for all times.

Then Odysseus' pitiless vengeance can be unleashed for the lightning massacre of the "suitors," the usurpers, and by the same token and no less fierce, of the servants who had betrayed their duty by making themselves their accomplices (*Odyssey* XXIII). The "suitors" are killed without exception and the guilty servants are hanged. Here, Homer no longer shows the chivalrous logic of loyal combat, but that of civil war which knows no limits. After which, supported by his father, Laertes, Odysseus will confront the troubles and the assembly of Ithaca, effecting the recognition of his legitimacy in using force and blood to restore the right of the City and the Kingdom (canto XXIV).[17]

---

17 This restoration of law by Odysseus has been emphasized by Eva Cantarella in *Ithaque. De la vengeance d'Ulysse à la naissance du droit* (Albin Michel, "Bibliothèque histoire" collection, 2003). Odysseus aims not so much to avenge himself as to "guarantee order within the group and affirm his role as chief." In France, more than 25 centuries after Homer, this is how young Louis XIII will still act during his 1617 coup d'état that allowed him to triumph over Concini and his followers.

The Poem of Penelope

The affirmed presence of Penelope also makes the *Odyssey* the poem of independent and respected femininity. When Penelope appears in the main hall of Ithaca's palace, tall and beautiful, her brilliant veils drawn over her cheeks, resembling golden Aphrodite, the "suitors'" knees give way and desire invades their hearts (*Odyssey* XVIII, 249).

Lover, wife, and mother, Penelope is in charge of the small kingdom of Ithaca in Odysseus' absence, a sign of the consideration given to femininity. No doubt one has not sufficiently remarked how "modern" is Penelope's fate. Destiny willed that, as a very young mother, she be deprived of her spouse for a long period during which she must assume, without any help, the weight of the kingdom and face the insistent, deceitful, violent schemes of the "suitors." In contemporary language, Penelope is the head of a single-parent family. She must raise alone a rather difficult son who is going through his adolescent crisis against her and plunges her into the worst torments. She is also the head of an enterprise (Ithaca) in the context of particularly trying conflicts. Finally, during the denouement, we will see her show remarkable mastery and prove capable of teaching Odysseus himself a thing or two about cunning.

Many other women are present in Homer. In the *Iliad*: Helen, Andromache, Hecuba, and Briseis. In the *Odyssey*: Helen again, Circe, Calypso, and the charming Nausicaa. But Penelope eclipses them all, except perhaps Helen, who is away. Constrained, like the women of our time, to inventing the art of remaining feminine in a social world dominated by masculine values, she often suffers, but she never gives up. She knows how to keep herself beautiful and desirable despite age. She also knows the importance of modesty for living in the society of men. When she is too tormented, she takes refuge in tears or sleep, allegorically watched over by Athena. Facing the greedy pack of "suitors," she does not engage the fight on the masculine terrain of violence. She uses cunning, smiles, invents the stratagem of weaving the cloth (her father-in-law Laertes' shroud), always to be redone, turning to her advantage the covetousness of which she is the object, and which perhaps does not displease her. However, upon the return of Odysseus, the most cunning of men, she somewhat deceives him, feigning not to recognize him, even after he has massacred the "suitors" with their son's help. He will first have to prove his identity through the ordeal of the secret of the conjugal bed, which he alone, with her, knows is immovable, having been carved from the unrootable trunk of an olive tree. Only then will she consent to give herself to him. In what sacred narrative of other cultures will one find an equivalent of Penelope and her complex femininity?

The Memory of a Lost Wisdom

In the *Odyssey*, the characters of Odysseus and Penelope live before us. Each episode of the return and reconquest of Ithaca imprints itself in memory. Take Odysseus' ruses, favored by Athena, to thwart the mistrust of the "suitors" (usurpers) who covet Penelope; how the hero makes himself recognized by his son Telemachus, and how they weave together the meticulous plan of vengeance; Odysseus' arrival at his palace, disguised as a beggar, whom only his old dog Argos recognizes and dies of joy. This friendly presence of the dog is nowhere to be encountered in the poems of the Near or Far East.

Shortly after, Odysseus is also recognized by his old nurse, Eurycleia, by the sight of an old scar, memory of a memorable boar hunt, the big game highly prized throughout Europe. And here now is Penelope, troubled, anxious, questioning. Then comes the rendering of just vengeance in an orgy of blood. Finally, reunion with Penelope will now be possible, after the ordeal of the secret of the conjugal bed that she imposes, not without cunning, on Odysseus. Then Athena intervenes, always attentive to her protégés. She delays the arrival of "rosy-fingered" Dawn so that the night of return lasts long…

Homer does not content himself with singing the memory of heroes. In the *Odyssey*, for example, the poet glorifies Eurycleia, Odysseus' old nurse, as well as Eumaeus, his swineherd, two characters which, while subordinate, are presented as examples for their intelligence and fidelity. We know how capital their role is alongside Odysseus in Ithaca's reconquest.

By virtue of Penelope's fertile presence, the *Odyssey* is also the poem of independent and respected femininity.

Like the heroes, true men seek the measure of their courage in combat and action, whereas women seek the light that makes them exist in love or self-sacrifice. It must be said again that the virtues sung by Homer are aesthetic. They are defined in regard to the beautiful and the ugly, the noble and the vile. But beauty is nothing without valor. Thus, Paris cannot be truly beautiful, since he is cowardly. On the other hand, Nestor, despite his age which now prevents him from fighting, retains the beauty of his courage by still being present at battle.

The Happy Society of Achilles' Shield

Behind the narrative of the two poems, a vision of the world and life also manifests itself, awakening the memory of a lost wisdom. In Homer, forests, rocks, and wild beasts have a soul. All of nature merges with the sacred and men are not cut off from it.

If Homer's world takes the cosmos as the model, it receives an ordered social description in the description of Achilles' shield forged by Hephaestus (*Iliad* XVIII). Two cities are represented there, one in peace, the other at war — the two faces of life. We discover that the Greek city to come, with its citizens, its institutions, its reciprocal duties, is already described in the poem. Hector explicitly says that he dies for the freedom of his homeland (*Iliad* VI, 455–528). Let us recall the end of *Odyssey*, when Odysseus has his right to execute the "suitors" and their accomplices recognized, so that the just order of the city may be reestablished. The foundation of social organization and civil peace is the ethnic unity of the city and respect for laws, guaranteed by the Elders and by force. Men are happy in a happy society, one that always resembles itself, where one marries as ancestors married, where one plows and harvests as one has always plowed and harvested. Individuals pass, but the city remains.

As Marcel Conche has emphasized, a society that can read its future in its past is a society at rest, without anxiety. The feeling of security is founded on this permanence. On the contrary, novelties and "progress" will bring trouble. From the moment one dreams up an ideal city and better tomorrows, the contentment is killed in each. From then on, the discontent of self and the world dominates. What is figured on Achilles' shield is, to the contrary, a happy society, full of the joy of living as it has always lived. Weddings are joyful, equity reigns, civic friendship is general. When war comes, the attacked city faces it, all the people go to the ramparts, the enemy has no ally inside.[18]

Anticipating Aristotle, Homer describes men as "political animals." In the *Iliad*, Homeric royalty is of the aristocratic and feudal type. It is the opposite of Oriental despotic monarchies. Agamemnon is not a despot or absolute sovereign. He is only first among his peers. Decision comes only after the consultation or deliberation of the Achaean chiefs assembled in council. With many variants and some violations, with unfortunate consequences, this model will remain dominant throughout European history, including in Rome during the imperial epoch. The occasional unworthy emperors will always have to deal with the senatorial aristocracy of the *patres*, which ensures the continuity of Romanity and power.

---

18 See Marcel Conche, *Essais sur Homère* (PUF, 1999); Eva Cantarella, *Ithaque. De la vengeance d'Ulysse à la naissance du droit* (Albin Michel, 2003); Anne-Marie Lecoq, *Le Bouclier d'Achille. Un tableau qui bouge* (Gallimard, 2010).

The Homeric Triad: Nature as Foundation

For the Ancients, Homer was "the beginning, the middle, and the end." A vision of the world and even a philosophy are implicitly deducible from his poems. Heraclitus summarized the cosmic foundation with a formulation very much his own: "The universe, the same for all beings, was created by no god nor by any man; but it has always been, is, and will be eternally living fire…"

The perception of an uncreated and ordered cosmos is accompanied by an enchanted vision conveyed by ancient myths. Myths are not beliefs, but images and energies manifesting the divine part in the world.

If observation of nature teaches the Greeks to measure their passions, to limit their desires, the idea they form of wisdom before Plato is without insipidity. They know that it is associated with fundamental harmonies born from overcome oppositions, masculine and feminine, violence and gentleness, instinct and reason. Heraclitus put himself in Homer's school when he stated that nature loved contraries and produced harmony out of them.

Thus, Homer bequeathed models and principles of life to future Europeans in the form of a triad: nature as foundation, excellence as goal, beauty as horizon.

Modern Europeans remain sensitive to the poetic vision of Nature conveyed by Homer. In it, in its immanence, here and now, they find answers to their anxieties, to the major questions of life and death: "As leaves are born, so are men. The leaves, in turn, the wind scatters on the ground and the verdant forest makes them born when the days of spring rise. So with men: one generation is born at the moment when another fades" (*Iliad* VI, 146).

In turn, generations fade to ensure the renewal of life. Such is the order of Nature. Each evening the sun disappears to be reborn each morning. Illness, old age and death, even that of a child, are natural data, perhaps cruel, but in no way dependent on the attention a god might give to each human among the few billion who populate the planet.

Homer, however, corrects the natural fatality of death by suggesting that mortals transmit something of themselves to those who will follow, and are thus assured of being a fragment of eternity. It is not merely a matter of transmission through filiation of descendants. Homer expresses many times the idea of memory left in remembrance. This is what Helen says in the *Iliad* (VI, 357–358): "Zeus has made us a hard destiny so that we may later be sung of by men to come."

Life and death weave the framework of these great poems, which suggest answers to the question of our finitude and to that of a "beautiful life," as the Stoics will understand it, in accordance with the order of the world.

In the *Odyssey*, the long and perilous voyage of return, a symbol of the reconquest of lost harmony, is punctuated with ordeals and traps. One of them is named Calypso, the gentle and ravishing nymph. She falls in love with the navigator to the point of wanting to keep him with her on her paradisiacal island forever. Odysseus does not resign himself to this lascivious prison. The desire to return haunts him beyond all seduction. Wishing to make him yield, in canto V of the *Odyssey* (203–220), Calypso then offers the impossible for a mortal. She offers him immortality and eternal youth, what others call paradise. And the incredible happens: in gallant terms, Odysseus refuses. He intends to assume his destiny as mortal, return to Ithaca and find Penelope there before dying at her side. Nothing would be worse than living forever far from his land and his people. The significance of this refusal continues to speak to us. Odysseus teaches that a life conforming to the order of nature, however cruel it may sometimes be, is superior to all mirages of immortality. "O my soul," Pindar will say, "do not aspire to eternal life, but exhaust the field of the possible."

Odysseus: The Refusal of Immortality

Odysseus has freed himself from the slavery of illusions. Free from chimeras, mirages, utopias, and temptations to escape his mortal destiny. Without death, there would be no life, no birth, no awakening, no renewal, no accomplishment.

Unlike animals who lack consciousness of death, men have this painful superiority of consciousness. Homer is so profoundly penetrated by this grandeur of human destiny that in canto XI of the *Odyssey*, he lets Odysseus descend to the kingdom of the dead and return, thus making him the only human to know this experience! Homer describes his encounter with Achilles' shade. And this shade weeps before him — not from simple regret for life, but because he has discovered that the kingdom of the dead, eternity, far from being a felicity, is of a "mortal" boredom.

In accordance with their imagination, every people and every religion have put forth an interpretation of what possibly comes after death. For the ancient Germanics and Vikings, warriors killed in combat — and they alone — found themselves afterwards at a banquet in Valhalla, facing some exchanges of arms between comrades. It is nice, but a bit repetitive. Christians, for their part, trusted the Bible and Jesus' implacable parable announcing damnation: "The angels will come forward and separate the wicked from the just to throw them into the burning furnace: there will be weeping and gnashing of teeth" (Matthew 13:47–50). This threat made generations of believers tremble. They hoped to be able to escape said furnace through various artifices, thinking that they would thus be given to contemplate the beauty of God or Jesus for eternity, which must be a bit tiresome. That's a long time, eternity... Muslims, in their dreams of a voluptuous beyond, believe that Allah reserves for each of his elect a harem of numerous houris, whose hymen would be reconstituted immediately after defloration. To each his interpretations...

Homer did not devise such unbridled nightmares or dreams. Despite Odysseus' descent to Hades, the idea that most often prevails with him is that once honors are rendered to a mortal's remains, he knows a definitive rest, a dreamless sleep without painful sojourn among the shades. This is, moreover, what Achilles himself suggested in canto IX of the *Iliad*: "The life of a man is not found again; never again does it let itself be taken or seized, from the day it has left the enclosure of his teeth…"

Death is not only the drama of which one tells, except for those who sincerely mourn the departed. It can be a deliverance. It puts an end to cruel illnesses, interrupts the decay of old age, and also yields place for new generations. Death can also prove to be a liberation when fate becomes too painful or dishonorable.

Excellence as Goal

Death, life… The chroniclers of our 15th century thus celebrated a young knight of Hainaut, Jacques de Lalaing, champion of lance and sword. Friend of the Duke of Burgundy, distinguished by Charles VII, coveted by ladies, he knew his first success in a joust in 1440. He was 19 years old. Invincible in tournaments, he was killed by a cannonball at the Battle of Poucques in 1453, a vintage retained to mark both the end of the Hundred Years' War and to date the fall of Constantinople. This epitaph was then written for him: "He was the flower of knights; he was beautiful like Paris the Trojan; he was pious like Aeneas; he was wise like Odysseus the Greek. When he found himself in battle against his enemies, he had the wrath of Hector the Trojan…" The comparison with Homer's heroes is revealing. Toward the end of our Middle Ages, after more than 20 centuries, the *Iliad* remained the standard of chivalry even though the transmission of the poem had experienced some vicissitudes.

Over the course of 20 centuries, nothing had truly changed in the fundamental "representations" of the best! Like the heroes of the *Iliad*, authentic men, noble and accomplished, strove for courage and sought in action the measure of their excellence, as women sought in love and self-sacrifice the light that makes them exist. For both, only what is beautiful and strong mattered. "Always be the best," Peleus recommended to his son Achilles, "prevail over all others" (*Iliad* VI, 208). When Penelope torments herself at the thought that her son could be killed by the "suitors," she especially fears that he might die "without glory," before having accomplished what would make him a hero equal to his father (*Odyssey* IV, 728). But aiming for excellence is not to be confused with vulgar competition for success, honors or money. Competition is not the goal. It is the stimulant. This difference allows one to distinguish between authenticity and its opposite, pride, vanity.

However, there remains a rather heavy ambiguity awakened by Peleus' already cited injunction to his son: "Prevail over all others..." The underlying idea of competition, even as a stimulant, implicitly establishes a confusion between excellence (interior virtue) and exploit (success tainted with vanity, even hubris). One thinks of the character of Alexander, incarnation of excess. Plutarch reports that during his campaigns the conqueror always kept under his pillow his sword and the *Iliad*. The image is beautiful, as it suggests that Alexander took Achilles, the impetuous hero, as his example, the pretext of his epic.

The exceptional character of the young conqueror of the immense Persian Empire draws attention to a constant trait of the European soul. Alexander was the living incarnation of the excess that ancient wisdom condemns and tries to correct. Excess, however, is an evident trait of the European character, a major trait, often catastrophic in its consequences, but inseparable from a tragic grandeur before which we are seized, torn between admiration and terror. Aeschylus and Sophocles made it one of the themes of their tragedies. And Homer? What does he say about it?

If one reflects on Achilles' character by carefully reading the *Iliad*, one discerns that Homer, while honoring the hero's ardor and courage, implicitly prefers Hector. We also know that Achilles becomes truly great not when he shows his superhuman force and excessive ardor, but when he returns Hector's remains to Priam through an unexpected trait of magnanimity due to the gods' intervention. Nor can we forget Homer's constant and implicit reprobation of excess, such as that of Agamemnon when he provokes Achilles' fatal anger, as well as the excess of this anger, which the failure of the three "wise men's" embassy in canto IX of the *Iliad* emphasizes by contrast.

Transcending Misfortune into Beauty

In the *Iliad* and the *Odyssey*, Homer tells of nobility facing the scourge of war. He tells of the courage of heroes who kill and die. He tells of Achilles' acceptance of his destiny, Hector's sacrifice as defender of his homeland, but also the pain of women (Hecuba or Andromache), the torments of an adolescent deprived of father (Telemachus), the dejection of old men (Priam). He tells of still many other things: the friendship uniting combatants (Achilles and Patroclus), the ambition of chiefs (Agamemnon and Achilles), their vanity, their quarrels. He tells of bravery and cowardice, love and tenderness. He tells of the taste for glory that raises men to the height of gods. He recalls that war irrevocably decides the fate of men, peoples and empires. This poem, where death is so present, also speaks of love for carnal life, rendered exuberant and all the more intense by being put at stake at every moment. The poem also celebrates the tragic courage that steels the heart before death, and makes one stronger than the gods. It says that the example of heroes continues to live on in the memory of the living.

The *Iliad* begins with Achilles' rage and ends with his appeasement before Priam's pain, whose son he has just killed. This is no mere matter of telling an epic and a drama in an admirable style. Homer is thus suggesting his lofty vision of life. If we know how to read and understand what we read, we discover little by little, like the Greeks of old, that he did not have a saccharine or moralizing interpretation of it. As the tragic poets will later say, he knew that evil can turn into good, as Sophocles shows in *Oedipus the King*, when, through Athena's intervention, the terrible Erinyes becomes the benevolent Eumenides.

In canto VIII of *The Odyssey*, Alcinous, king of the Phaeacians, offers hospitality to Odysseus. Before the king, he listens to the bard Demodocus sing the episode of the Trojan horse that allowed the Achaeans to seize the city. Odysseus is overwhelmed by the recollection of the war of old, when so many of his own died. He struggles to hide his tears. Alcinous understands his emotion, but he presents an interpretation of the combatants' destiny that transfigures it: "If the gods have inflicted death on so many men, it is to give songs to people of the future" (VIII, 579–580). To "give songs," or in other words, poems — this means transcending misfortune into a work of art and into beauty. Misfortune is thus reversed into its opposite.

This transcendence is constant in Homer and it is, without a doubt, the strongest thing he bequeaths to us for confronting life. The goddess invoked in the first verses of the *Iliad* is the Muse of memory and poetry. She inspires Homer and gives him the power to transmute "fatal anger" into a work of art. The first stanzas thus invite meditation on the contribution of tragic wisdom that despises complaint and excess of compassion. Through the grace of the work of art, the worst ("fatal anger") can be transformed into good, that is to say, into beauty. One finds a similar transformation in numerous later works of European literature, for example *The Romance of Tristan and Isolde*, *Hamlet*, or, once again, *The Princess of Clèves*. The more cruel the destiny, the greater it is, the more beautiful it is. Here, Homer accomplishes in a striking manner the aesthetic reversal operated by the tragic spirit. He awakens in us a thirst for heroism and beauty. One must remember this when one finds oneself confronted with misfortunes born of war or the hazards of existence.

Neither Dogma Nor Moralizing Discourse

One can never say it enough: Homer shows but does not explain, does not conceptualize, as I have just risked doing. Thus he does with the gods, suggesting that men should expect nothing from them, and pin hope on no other resource than themselves. Hector says this clearly by rejecting the sinister omen of disaster: "There is only one good omen, it is to fight for one's homeland" (*Iliad* XII, 243). During the final battle, having understood that he is condemned by the gods and destiny, Hector tears himself from despair through a surge of tragic heroism: "Well! No, I do not intend to die without struggle nor without glory, nor without some high deed whose account will reach men to come" (XXII, 304–305). One finds this message's echo very strong in all epochs of European history, an echo which so often magnifies the hero's desire for excellence, especially the unfortunate hero, magnified by death in combat and the epic defeat of his camp, as witnessed by the accounts of famous battles — Thermopylae, Roncevaux, Camerone, and Dien Bien Phu.

If they sing excellence, the great poems are exempt from dogmas and moral discourse. Neither Fall, nor Salvation, nor sin, nor confession, nor guilt, nor self-accusation. They ignore the existence of metaphysical Evil. The virtues sung by Homer are not moral but aesthetic. There is no prohibition linked to sex, pleasure, or force, only the sense of measure and reciprocal commitments — Hector and Andromache, Odysseus and Penelope…

Homer believes in the unity of the human being sealed by his acts, which he magnifies through his style. Men are therefore defined in regard to the beautiful and the ugly, the noble and the vile.

Or, to put it differently, the effort towards beauty is the condition of good. But beauty is nothing without loyalty or valor.

To Europeans, the founding poet recalls that they were not born yesterday. He bequeaths them the foundation of their identity, the first perfect expression of an ethical and aesthetic patrimony that he himself held in inheritance and that he has sublimated in a way one would call divine. The principles he brought to life through his characters have not ceased to be reborn up to us, all the while showing that the secret thread of our tradition could not be broken. Thus, the future takes root in the memory of the past.

CHAPTER VI

OUR HIDDEN WISDOM

L EARNING TO live well and die well was the great concern of the Stoics. The ethics of these athletes of will is common to men and women, in the past as well as in recent periods. For there exists a Stoicism and even a feminine heroism that is not of war. The daily heroism of women, another word for Stoicism, is what conventional discourse speaks of least. And yet one must be blind not to see it behind the energy that is needed for the constant tasks that ensure the perpetual rebirth of life and are the essence of femininity.

The Young Unknown Woman of Berlin

One of the most striking contemporary testimonies of feminine Stoicism has been offered to us by the Dantesque memories of a young German woman during the tragic days of her country's defeat, in Berlin, in 1945. In accordance with her will, her memories remain anonymous — one understands why after reading them, and this inspires admiration. Published in English as early as 1954, these memories were the subject of a new edition in 2003, two years after the author's death, whose identity was then revealed. A French translation appeared in 2006 under the title *A Woman in Berlin: Journal, April 20–June 22, 1945*.[1]

---

1   Text translated by Françoise Wuilmart and presented by Hans Magnus Enzensberger (Gallimard, "Témoins" collection; "Folio" collection, 2008).

A young apolitical German journalist, certainly lively and pretty, who traveled extensively for her work and spoke a little Russian, was caught, like so many other women, in the fatal trap that Berlin had become at the end of April 1945, during the collapse of the Reich and the arrival of Russian troops. There were no more men in the great city, except for a few old men. All the others were dead or mobilized elsewhere in the final battles. The young Berliner then suffered the fate of all women who were caught in this sinister hell: repeated rapes accompanied by manifold violence from brutal soldiers, drunk on vodka, victory, and revenge. Without water, without services, and without food, the city, demolished by bombings, had returned to the Stone Age.

The young anonymous woman recounts her fate and that of other women around her. Terror and horror are described hour by hour. But often with a touch of humor and tonic detachment. "Overcoming death makes one stronger" — this remark appears several times throughout her journal. Indeed, she survived everything, physically and morally. And this victory over fate and misfortune is undoubtedly the most admirable part of this pity-evoking book. The reader is seized with horrified compassion as much as with admiration. Rarely has such a poignant and truthful testimony been written from the depths of hell. In these ordeals, after days of panic and horror, after the rapes and all the repugnant things she endured like so many others, this young woman achieved a sort of Stoic serenity. This journal of terror manifests indestructible vigor, courage, and tonicity. One perceives that this young woman was saved in part by having secretly kept her journal each day on the remains of a wretched notebook or simple scraps of paper. Thus returning to herself, freeing herself through the catharsis of writing, she never abandoned herself. "We need spiritual nourishment," she notes. Being detached from all religion, she finds this nourishment in herself and in her culture. Lucid, she writes: "I know now that we Germans are finished, but our good old sun still shines in the sky." And elsewhere: "I know that I am part of my people, even now." No self-pity in her. The defeat and what accompanied it did not crush her and did not cancel her capacity to think. Her inner freedom resisted everything. If ever an implicit Stoicism found expression, it is here.

An Extreme Wisdom

I have said "implicit" in speaking of the Stoicism of the young anonymous woman of Berlin. But to act on the soul, the implicit nevertheless deserves to be meditated upon. The journal of hell kept by the young Berliner helped her to do so. This is what one expects from any intense experience that brings spirituality into play, a sometimes equivocal word, yet one which is not confused with the supernatural, but rather is frontally opposed to brute materiality. In a word, sex belongs to materiality, love to spirituality.

The awakening and deepening of spirituality, so present in the young anonymous woman of Berlin, are favored by the reading and meditation of predisposed minds, those called sages, religious, spiritual, or philosophical reformers. They never emerge from nothingness or without reason. Homer, Epictetus, Confucius, Buddha, Jesus, Luther, or Nietzsche could only appear and arouse a strong echo in their time, following certain events along with a certain demand and collective fermentation. A prophet or reformer is always the result of the encounter between an exceptional mind and the expectations of an era. They are relayed by awakeners who have a decisive role, even when history does not retain their name.

The academic Pierre Hadot[2] (1922–2010) was one of these awakeners who left a mark in the history of ideas and spirituality. In an

---

2   He and I shared mutual esteem. I published a long interview with him, conducted by Pauline Lecomte, in *La Nouvelle Revue d'Histoire* no. 22 (January 2006). And we exchanged a sustained correspondence. He took up some of my reflections in his book *The Veil of Isis*.

unforeseeable way, he initiated a reversal of perspectives on the subject of ancient philosophy and Stoicism.

He arrived at the right moment for his qualities to meet an expectation that was not limited to scholars.

Longtime holder of the chair of the history of ancient thought at the Collège de France, Pierre Hadot was not an academic like the others. He was an incomparable scholar, but he was inhabited by his subject to the point of having himself become a philosopher in the ancient sense of the word. From reading his books, one can emerge changed.

Whether he dealt with Marcus Aurelius or Plotinus, Stoicism or Neoplatonism, Pierre Hadot showed with limpid erudition that philosophy for the Ancients was not a construction of systems, but a choice of life.[3] He emphasized that a philosopher in Antiquity was not a professor in the modern sense of the word, repeating without investing himself. Nor was he a theoretician of philosophy. A philosopher of Antiquity was someone who lived as a philosopher, as a "friend of wisdom."

In one of his books, Pierre Hadot recalled the destiny of Cato of Utica, statesman of the 1st century before our era, a contemporary and adversary of Caesar, which was to lead him, after the defeat of his side, to one of the most famous suicides of Antiquity. Cato, he says, was a Stoic philosopher, yet he wrote no philosophical work. But he lived and died as a Stoic.[4] In the eyes of the masters of ancient philosophy, the authentic philosopher is not one who dissertates on theories, comments on authors, invents concepts or writes books, but rather is one who lives according to the wisdom that ancient philosophy teaches.

---

3   Pierre Hadot, *La Philosophie comme manière de vivre*, interviews with Jeannie Carlier and Arnold J. Davidson (Albin Michel, 2001).

4   Pierre Hadot, *La Citadelle intérieure. Introduction aux "Pensées" de Marc Aurèle* (Fayard, 1997), p. 16.

This interpretation, constantly present in Pierre Hadot since his inaugural lecture at the Collège de France,[5] brought about a change of perspective. He made it understood that ancient philosophers did not engage in theoretical activities locked in a narcissistic ivory tower. He showed that, for them, being Epicurean, Stoic, or Neoplatonic implied an exercise upon oneself, a spiritual transformation and a modification of behavior whose effects on the soul are analogous to those that training produces on an athlete's body: self-control in Stoicism, or renunciation of superfluous pleasures in Epicureanism. As Epictetus says, the Stoic who had the most influence on Emperor Marcus Aurelius (III, 21, 5): "Eat like a man, drink like a man, dress yourself, marry, have children, lead a citizen's life… Show us this, so that we may know if you have truly learned something from the philosophers."

A Very Current School of Life

The change of perspective introduced by Pierre Hadot also made it possible to understand that the way of living that appeared in Greece and Rome several centuries before our era does not belong to the past. It is not an ancient affair, but a way of life that still concerns us. The desire to conduct oneself well by practicing an "extreme" wisdom has endured through time, despite Christianity, which strove to relate everything to its system, to the beyond and to the Scriptures. As early as the 2nd century of our era, several illustrious Christians, Clement of Alexandria and Origen, put themselves to school with Stoicism. Their intention was not to become Stoics. But they had recognized in the spiritual exercises of the disciples of Zeno, Epictetus, and Marcus Aurelius models for the deepening of thought. If they studied Stoicism, it was to make philosophy the servant of theology (*philosophica ancilla theologica*), as St. Thomas Aquinas would say: to put the intellectual instruments of philosophy at the service of

---

5 Pierre Hadot, *Éloge de la philosophie antique. Leçon inaugurale au Collège de France, le 18 février 1983* (Éditions Allia, 1997).

theology. Thus, while declaring themselves adversaries of Stoicism, certain Church Fathers from the 2nd to the 4th century, such as Irenaeus, Tertullian, and Athanasius, nevertheless became its diffusers through the multiple quotations that stud their works.[6] They are the ones who introduced Seneca into Christian thought even while criticizing him.

Always present during the Middle Ages, and notably within chivalry,[7] Stoicism made a strong comeback with the Renaissance, which saw the flourishing of translations of Epictetus and Marcus Aurelius, then with the works of the neo-Stoics of the 16th and 17th centuries, Justus Lipsius, Guillaume du Vair, and Corneille. From then on, the polemic opened by St. Augustine to oppose the City of men to the City of God lost much of its force. It is here and now that one has to build one's life rather than in anticipation of a hypothetical "beyond" with alternating promises of paradise and threats of damnation. The desire for wisdom on Earth supplanted hope for Salvation in another world. Such a choice speaks to us.

The Epicureans and Stoics showed that all the misfortunes of men came from an inability to "make the present well." In other words, they taught how to live well in immanence by ceasing to be haunted by the anxieties of the beyond.

This is what Goethe suggests in his second *Faust* when, through the face-to-face between Homer's Helen and Faust, he stages the encounter of ancient beauty and modern man. In the manner of the Greeks, Goethe wished to reinvent "the fullness of the moment" which would be like an eternity. A reinvention from which we, modern men and women, benefit when we show ourselves worthy of it, in love as in all the intense moments of life.

---

6   Jacqueline Lagrée, *Le Néostoïcisme* (Vrin, 2010), p. 13–14; Lucien Jerphagnon, *Les Armes et les mots* (Robert Laffont, "Bouquins", 2012), part 2 on "The Divine Caesars," chapters IV, V, VI).

7   Martin Aurell, introduction to the collective volume *Chevalerie et christianisme aux xiie et xiiie siècles* (Presses universitaires de Rennes, 2012).

Before Nietzsche, Goethe had reinvented the great "yes" to life, imagining a new spiritual gaze in response to the nihilism of his time. He fulfilled an expectation that has only continued to grow ever more after him.

From Myths to Philosophy

In its variations, ancient philosophy was born out of the ancient myths that preceded it. It was born from Homer while sometimes claiming to surpass him. Ever since there has been reflection on the meaning of myths, we no longer confuse them with legends or fantastic stories. We have understood that myths are in fact the words of the origin (*arché*), powerful images and energies, not concepts. They are polysemous images which incite a multidimensional interpretation of the world, often richer and deeper than those conveyed by philosophies. The most ancient myths say what cannot be said: the beginning of the world of which there are no witnesses, the origins of the cosmic void that the ancient Greeks called *Khaos*. Present in Homer and Hesiod, myths also respond to a fundamental question that philosophers up to the Stoics then took up with more or less success: what is a "beautiful" life or a "good" life for mortals?

These were not dogmatic or moral interrogations: they concerned the meaning of life and death. The answers that Homer formulated were the desire for excellence, tragic courage in the face of ineluctable destiny, the transmutation of misfortune into beauty… He also responded by forcefully expressing just how important for the individual is the vital feeling of belonging to a people or a city that precedes and survives him. Through this belonging, individuals cease to be separated.

Gathering ancient myths in an ordered formulation, Hesiod in his time also brought answers to the great interrogations, in a form that ancient philosophy essentially took up. In the *Theogony*, he recounts the birth of life emerging from the original abyss — *Khaos*. He describes the first and complementary couples: Gaia and Ouranos, Earth and starry Sky, black Night and the Light of Day, Earth and Waves.

The powers of chaotic excess are personified by the divinities of night, while those of order and measure are by the diurnal divinities. One can note that the generative processes thus described find a striking echo in the theories constructed by today's astrophysicists...

After the coupling of Gaia with Ouranos, whom she had engendered alone — this is, therefore, the first manifestation of sexuation — the Titan Kronos intervenes and emasculates his father (Ouranos) to disjoin him from Gaia. Thus was effected the fundamental distinction between masculine and feminine. Then a new principle of order comes to impose itself when Zeus revolts against Kronos, his father who devoured his children. As Paul Mazon wrote in his *Introduction to Hesiod's Theogony*: "The mysterious force that gives birth to life, if nothing comes to regulate and contain it, creates only confusion and death." Like Kronos who swallowed his children, "it immediately destroys what it has just brought into the world."[8] Such is the meaning of the myth of Ouranos mutilated and separated from Gaia by Kronos, then of Kronos and the Titans dominated by Zeus. This victory of the new solar divinities incarnating the Olympian order over the chthonic divinities of earth and night perhaps translates, in a mythical register, what was the conquest of Hellas by the ancestors of the Achaeans who dominated the protohistoric populations devoted to the cult of the Earth-Mother.

At the end of these battles, the world is thus shared in an ordered manner: to Gaia is accorded the Earth, to Ouranos the Sky, to Poseidon the sea. What is thus outlined in the space of thought is the idea of "cosmos," the idea that the universe is not chaos, but that it is, to the contrary, subject to order and harmony. It is not a moral world responding to the desires of imploring and anguished men in pursuit of

---

8   Paul Mazon, *Introduction à la Théogonie d'Hésiode* (Les Belles Lettres, 1928).

justice and goodness. It is the world of Nature, beautiful, mysterious, ordered, and dangerous.

Greek philosophy subsequently strove to rationalize the religious message of myth. In essence, the Stoics would say that a "beautiful" or "good" life is a life in harmony with the cosmic order. This is already what was expressed in veiled form in the poetic narrative in the *Iliad* and the *Odyssey*. Living in harmony with the cosmic order is accompanied by the feeling of belonging to a privileged city where one was born. Very early on, this gave birth to the idea of homeland, which one finds for the first time in Homer, in the *Iliad*, when the poet designates a character's country of birth (*patrida*), or as homeland in the sense we understand it when Hector speaks of his resolution to "fight for his homeland" (*Iliad* XII, 243). The homeland is the idealized hearth that merges with the city's destiny. It is the sacred land where ancestors rest. Three hundred years after Homer, Aeschylus in his tragedy *The Persians*, describing the battle of Salamis (in 480 before our era), addresses the Greeks to encourage them to repel the invaders: "Deliver the homeland, your children, your women, the dwellings of the gods and the tombs of your ancestors! Now, this is the supreme battle!" The poet Horace, a contemporary of Augustus, still understood this nearly four centuries later, such as in his famous injunction: "*Dulce et decorum est pro patria mori!*" (It is sweet and beautiful to die for the homeland).[9]

The Inner Citadel

When it comes to Stoicism, the great affair of Antiquity, we must establish a differentiation between the substance of this philosophy and what is commonly called "Stoicism." In common parlance, to say of someone that he is "stoic" means that he faces ordeals with a firm heart, without complaining and groaning. This was not primarily the

---

9   Horace, *Odes*, Book III, 2 (Les Belles Lettres, 1954), p. 97.

self-mastery that Stoic philosophy aimed at, even if it was its most fortunate consequence.

Like Epicureanism, but by other means, Stoicism wanted to be a recipe for happiness, a eudemonism for purely personal use, without any proselytism. It rested on the idea that wisdom commands one to free themselves from all desire and all passion, the causes of troubles. It replaced the pleasure principle with the principle of reason. It knew that the most delicious drink can turn into poison... But, unlike the followers of Christianity, when the Stoics recommended refusing luxury, this was not in the name of a morality of abstinence, but rather to train oneself to not be dependent on wealth. Far from opposing happiness and virtue, they saw in the second the condition of the first.

To take up Pierre Hadot's formulation, the Stoic Emperor Marcus Aurelius, in writing his *Meditations*, built within himself an inner citadel inaccessible to troubles and passions. But this citadel, where serenity reigns in principle, is not closed to the world. On the contrary, it is a base of operations that allows one to see and act from afar. The *Meditations* form the book of a man of action who seeks serenity because it is the indispensable condition of efficacy. Thus, the emperor strives to practice the three fundamental disciplines of Stoicism defined by Epictetus: judgment, desire, and action.

Marcus Aurelius spent part of his life warring to protect the Empire from the onslaught of the Barbarians. He even died on the Danube frontier on March 17, 181, at the current location of Vienna that would subsequently so often be disputed by Asian conquerors. It was at the bivouac, in a dangerous and uncomfortable situation, between two battles, during operations conducted in 170–173 against the Quadi, that he wrote his famous *Meditations*, or "Matters for Myself," a model of spiritual meditations intended for self-improvement.[10]

---

10 Pierre Hadot vigorously contests a psychological interpretation by Renan, otherwise an admirer of the Stoic emperor, which gave birth to the tenacious myth that made Marcus Aurelius into a depressive pessimist and a disillusioned man,

As Marcus Aurelius' example shows, Stoicism was understood and lived as an inner discipline and school of courage. The path leading to self-mastery found its supreme application in impassivity before death. Learning to die well was the great affair of Stoicism. The Romans, masters of will, were not mistaken. Before death — especially voluntary death — it was to the Stoics that they turned.

They are the ones who made suicide the philosophical act par excellence, a human privilege refused to the gods, as Pliny the Elder says: "Even God cannot do everything: he cannot give himself death, even if he wanted to, the most beautiful privilege he has granted to man amidst all the evils of life."

Spontaneously Stoic, firm, and courageous in adversity in the manner of Cato or Seneca, the "old Romans" practiced voluntary death as the Japanese samurai would do much later. The women who resorted to such were also numerous, notably the legendary Lucretia, whose suicide in 509 before our era gave the signal for revolt against the Etruscan monarchy.

One may remember that in Rome, many Stoics were also statesmen and men of war, first and foremost among them Emperor Marcus Aurelius who was on campaign, sword in hand, on the Danube for about ten years. There were many others as well: Junius Rusticus, twice consul under Marcus Aurelius and his master in Stoicism, Claudius Maximus, proconsul of Africa in the same period, Cicero to a certain extent, Arrian of Nicomedia, Seneca, and Cato of Utica, of course.

Since its foundation by Zeno under a portico of Athens around 300 before our era, the Stoic school had not ceased to evolve and enrich itself in Greece and then in Rome. Without being a religion, it wanted to be more than a simple philosophy. It wanted to be a total wisdom that Epictetus and his disciple Arrian, a general, statesman, and philosopher, undertook to codify. Arrian took up the pen (or stylus) to write in the most concise and vigorous way possible the *Manual* that

---

whereas everything shows that he was full of vigor. See *La Citadelle intérieure*, op. cit., p. 263 ff.

bears Epictetus' name.[11] The Greek title of this famous little opuscule, *Enkhiridion*, also means dagger. Like a dagger, this manual was made to be kept at hand in all circumstances.

Born in Phrygia around the year 50 of our era, Epictetus, the philosopher with the dagger, applied his principles in his own life. A freed slave, poor and lame, he managed through effort, reason, and will to equal the best, if not the gods. He was inhabited by the desire for excellence. In his youth, he was witness to the Stoic renewal by which part of the Roman aristocracy, weary of corruption, sought to establish a moral recovery after Nero. Epictetus did not yield to the illusory hope of changing the world order. His desire or ambition was to improve himself personally, to be an example. And he was.

What Depends on Us

The first principle of Stoicism is coherence. Zeno described the sovereign good thusly: "To live in a coherent manner, that is to say, to live according to a unified and harmonious rule of life."

The second great principle of Stoicism can be summated as being "indifference to indifferent things." Everything that does not depend on our freedom (poverty, wealth, health, illness) is neither good nor bad in itself, it is indifferent. One must therefore free oneself from it.

Even in chains and under torture, Epictetus assures that we can remain masters of our representations as long as we will such. Good and evil depend on us, since they consist in the idea we form of them. Thus, Epictetus taught indifference toward external events. He believed that there is only lived wisdom, and no other teaching than example. The virtues celebrated by the *Manual* are not fatalism, but courage, endurance, decency, measure, and benevolence. On the other hand, pity and

---

11   There exist several translations in French in pocket collections, accompanied by often whimsical commentaries. For an in-depth study, one should refer to Pierre Hadot's edition, *Manuel d'Épictète* (Le Livre de Poche, "Classiques de poche," 2000).

humility are ignored. Struck on the right cheek, Epictetus does not turn the left cheek to his aggressor.

In his *Thoughts*, Pascal discerned in Epictetus' teaching "the principles of a diabolical pride." If evil is only an opinion, if happiness depends on our will, man can make his own salvation, and his "misery" is denied. This pretension is indeed incompatible with the Christian idea of the "Fall" and "Salvation."

Recommending that we free ourselves from "things that do not depend on us," the first precept of Epictetus' *Manual*, key to the edifice, establishes a principle on which to base one's freedom. It receives the commentary of precept XIX: "Only one road leads to freedom, contempt for what does not depend on us." The proud formulation of precept LIII, the last, is even more vigorous: "So-and-so can kill me, not harm me." Let us replace "harm me," which is improper, with "reach me." Here we are at the heart of the question. One can kill me, but not reach me in my soul, because I have made it invulnerable, inviolable.

"I am not my body, nor the involuntary emotions that can move it," Epictetus says again. From this detachment toward the body and emotions, the Stoics drew the idea of their freedom.

Not everything is of the same ink in the *Manual*. Pushed to the extreme, Epictetus' Stoicism sometimes turns against what it drains of best. The school of absolute detachment carries within it a sometimes absurd principle. Once one has truly detached oneself from everything, from *élan*, ardor, passion, fantasy, sympathy, and altruism, what remains? A dried-up being, an arid soul.

Nor can one ignore what is irritating in certain paradoxes. In embracing your wife and your children, for example, the *Manual* advises that you must think about how you are embracing a mortal being: "If he dies, you will not be troubled…" We are here in full logical delirium! The intoxication of reasoning thus leads to perfect absurdity, as in this syllogism by Zeno: "No evil is glorious; yet death is glorious; therefore death is not an evil." But one finds many deductions just as specious or absurd in Plato's dialogues: "No one wants to harm himself, therefore all evil occurs involuntarily, for the bad man harms himself…" The foolishness of this kind of reasoning puts us on guard against the ridiculous excesses of abstraction. One can therefore stick to Epictetus' fundamental precept, which is itself truly a bearer of wisdom: to distinguish between what we can act upon and what does not depend on our will — to which we must therefore remain indifferent.

The Accord of Thoughts and Acts

Because it proposes to its followers a series of precepts which allow them to achieve happiness, in the Greek sense of the word (an admired ideal[12]), by freeing themselves from the impact that the sufferings and disappointments of existence can have, Stoicism might seem flatly utilitarian.

But a nobler finality is implicitly outlined: the mastery of oneself through the discipline of impulses and actions.

Apparently, it is undoubtedly easier to adopt the Stoic wisdom of detachment when one has nothing or when one is a slave. Like the sick person who implores divine mercy, one can draw from this wisdom a principle of consolation that helps bear one's state. In Emperor Marcus Aurelius, to whom were offered all the promises of power, wealth, and authority, it was otherwise. In him, the asceticism of detachment and the scrupulous concern for good broached heroism. And one can retain as a precious maxim this thought of the Stoic emperor: "If everything is subject to chance, do not be yourself an object of chance."

Marcus Aurelius considered the sometimes revolting aspects of existence as the ineluctable consequences of Nature's will, assimilated to the idea of a universal Reason. This form of fatalism departs from the revolt that Homer witnesses before an unjust fate. In the *Iliad*, for

---

12   In his essay preceding the edition of Seneca's *On the Tranquility of the Soul*, published by Rivages in 1988 (p. 55, note 15), Paul Veyne recalls that, for Aristotle, living "happily" means living in accordance with an ideal conception of the citizen and the city.

example, the poet lends these words to Apollo when he is indignant at Hector's death decided by the gods: "You, gods, are cruel and maleficent!" In the meantime, Plato's moralism had left its mark on Stoicism, setting aside Homer's tragic spirit, to which Nietzsche would return in his way, as Pierre Hadot implicitly notes: "Between Stoicism and Nietzsche, an abyss opens up. While the Stoic 'yes' is a consent to the rationality of the world, the Dionysian affirmation of existence that Nietzsche speaks of is a 'yes' given to irrationality, to the blind cruelty of life, to the will to power beyond good and evil."[13]

Ancient Stoicism wanted to be above all an individual wisdom, a school of discipline and inner serenity that kept at a distance "what does not depend on us" and therefore prepared one to be available for the service of the *res publica*. Hence, many Stoics exercised high functions in Rome. Without being a properly speaking "political philosophy" aimed at organizing the city, Stoicism, because it demanded of its followers courage, endurance, patience, and magnanimity, was a high school where civic and aristocratic virtues were acquired. Emperor Marcus Aurelius incarnated these virtues in his acts just as much as in his writings.

The Stoics in the City

On several occasion in his *Meditations*, Marcus Aurelius illustrates a portrait of the ideal prince, taking as the example his adoptive father, Antoninus Pius. He describes the moral qualities which this emperor, whom he proposes to imitate, demonstrated in his way of governing. "When a decision was made, Antoninus stuck to it firmly. He was of even temper, he did not seek to humiliate, but feared and despised no one. He led a simple life, contenting himself with little for his dwelling, his bed, his clothes, his food, his domesticity."[14] For Marcus Aurelius,

---

13   Pierre Hadot, op. cit., p. 162.

14   Pierre Hadot, op. cit., p. 319.

philosophy does not propose a political program, but it can form and prepare the statesman for the disciplines of action.

What depends on us… Epictetus made this maxim into a major axiom of his teaching.

It had not been within the power of the philosopher with the dagger to reform the Empire after Nero. And this was never his ambition. But making his life a model in accord with his thoughts did depend on him. In the following generation, these thoughts had a decisive influence on Marcus Aurelius. This memory offers matter for meditation on the path of examples and ideas.

Among the accusations made against the Stoics, one cannot forget that of a certain cosmopolitanism. Indeed, in the pen of Marcus Aurelius (*Meditations*) or Seneca (*On the Tranquility of the Soul*), one can sometimes read statements that would suggest this: "We consider the entire world as our homeland…" But one must read the rest: "… so that our valor may have more field to exercise itself." This modifies the first meaning and sounds rather like a satisfied imperialism that can make good accommodation with patriotism. Let us quote Seneca again: "Certain goods, for the Stoics, are of first order," he says, notably "the salvation of the homeland." But it is accurate that the Stoics held all men to be their fellow beings, including foreigners and Barbarians, which implied that one show benevolence toward them, except in situations of conflict. Thus, alongside his declarations of universal benevolence, Seneca does not hesitate to praise the "wisdom" of Scipio, the pitiless destroyer of Carthage. One can add that, in the pen of Latin and Greek philosophers, the concept of "man" is most often an abstraction behind which is the profile of a very concrete reality. When they say "men," they are not thinking of humanity in general. They think of Greeks or Romans, free, virtuous citizens endowed with reason. In this respect, the Europeans of the Enlightenment resembled them inasmuch as "men" implicitly meant Europeans.

The Neo-Stoicism of *The Princess of Clèves*

From age to age, one sees examples of Stoicism, or rather neo-Stoicism, resurge in Europe, for it aligns with the state of mind already present in the Homeric poems. Stoicism was a school of self-mastery and firmness of soul, but it sometimes fled from life. The new Stoicism, which one sees appearing in the 17th century, teaches firmness of soul just as much, but it is new insofar as it confronts the world without fleeing from its tragic part. Following Nietzsche's word, it is a "yes" to life.

One such accomplished example of neo-Stoicism took place during the Grand Siècle in *The Princess of Clèves*, a brief novel published anonymously by Madame de La Fayette in 1678, when Louis XIV had been governing personally for 17 years. It was during her liaison with the Duke of La Rochefoucauld that she wrote this novel, whose imprint and style left a mark on French letters, being a concentrated work entirely centered around the movements of the heart, such as those of which Corneille had written.

The plot of *The Princess of Clèves* was inspired by certain real facts of its time. Let us recall: at the court of King Henry II, the very young Mademoiselle de Chartres is noticed by the Prince of Clèves, who falls in love with her and asks for her hand in marriage, which she accepts as a marriage of reason. Barely married, at a ball she falls madly in love with the young and handsome Duke of Nemours. The two young people see each other often at court and, despite the violence of their feelings, they remain silent. Soon, following several adventures, young Madame de Clèves can no longer bear this secret. In all innocence and misunderstanding certain confidences from her husband, she confesses to him that she is in love with another man, but she swears to him that she will always remain faithful to him. Through an indiscretion, the prince discovers the name of his rival. Seized with violent jealousy, Monsieur de Clèves has the Duke of Nemours watched. He learns that the latter spent two nights in his wife's park when she retired to the countryside. Nothing happened. But, believing himself deceived, the

Prince of Clèves dies of shock. Having become free, Madame de Clèves confesses her feelings to the Duke of Nemours during an interview, but she refuses to marry him since he is the cause of her husband's death. Despite all the supplications, she retires, never to appear in the world again, and dies in solitude, "leaving examples of inimitable virtue."

What has never ceased to attract and move in this short novel is the mad passion that unites and separates two young people drawn together by love. All of this is expressed with admirable precision and accuracy. But what is striking is the extent to which the heroes preserve their dignity in the midst of the disorder of feelings. The most striking character is that of the young Madame de Clèves. She is the sister of the Cornelian heroines who want to dominate their passion in the name of the idea they have of honor. She does not withdraw from life, since she listens to the Duke of Nemours and even confesses her love to him. But she refuses to abdicate her pride. She no doubt rightly fears falling under the power of a seducer who would soon dishonor and make her suffer. This anguish is joined with the will to do nothing that might tarnish her intimate pride and taint her with remorse. By concluding this novel with the proud refusal of the Princess of Clèves, Madame de La Fayette made an offering to the neo-Stoicism of her time, which her friend La Rochefoucauld nevertheless condemned in the name of another morality, that of Jansenism.

The Condemnation of the Jansenists

The bitter loser of the Fronde, the Duke of La Rochefoucauld had distanced himself from the enthusiasms of his youth. A complex mind, which Retz confessed himself powerless to fathom, he had rejected the ancient chivalrous morality of his milieu. In his mature age, after the failure of his ambitions, this morality appeared to him as bearing illusions or even impostures. In his *Maxims*, he came to condemn heroic ethics as a dissimulation of selfish interests. His position of withdrawal from the world and aristocratic values look like another Fronde pursued by other means and for other purposes.

In the Jansenist circles he frequented, La Rochefoucauld encountered the Augustinian philosophy that prevailed among them. I have already evoked the thesis that St. Augustine upholds in *The City of God*: "Two cities have been formed by two loves: the earthly by the love of self, even to the contempt of God; the heavenly by the love of God, even to the contempt of self." This manifesto gave the faithful the model of the City of God so that they could turn away from the seductions and sins of the earthly city. The sharp Manichaeism that opposed the heavenly city to that of men, as much as love of God associated with contempt for self, implies a condemnation of self-love, honor, and chivalrous pride. If man could find wisdom and happiness by doing without Christ, what good would the Incarnation be? It was therefore necessary that the virtues of the Stoics, the athletes of moral tension, should be mere false virtues, since they were not inspired by Christ. The asceticism of the Stoics was only pride.

This Augustinian and Jansenist condemnation of Stoic virtues is found in the *Maxims*, from the frontispiece which claims to tear from Seneca the mask of his impassivity to reveal what would be his secret disarray. La Rochefoucauld thus embraced one of the quarrels of his time, that which questioned one of the great contributions of the Renaissance: humanism as a synthesis of Christian thought and ancient thought. This question had been debated at length at the Council of Trent. For his part, La Rochefoucauld took rank among those who rejected Stoic wisdom and took up St. Augustine's affirmation: "The virtues of the infidels (pagans) are vices."[15]

---

15 Jean Lafond, preface to *Réflexions ou Sentences et Maximes morales de La Rochefoucauld* (Gallimard, 1976).

A Samurai Morality

Some of the duke's contemporaries, notably Madame de Schomberg, questioned his about-face. Might not the author of the *Maxims* have wanted in reality to secretly justify the condemnation of all virtues by libertine philosophers (atheists)? Should not the moralist in turn be unmasked? Did not the Augustinian categories serve to smuggle in an unavowable morality such as that Molière staged in his *Don Juan* in 1665?

The one certainty in this debate was that the duke had not succeeded in convincing his friend Madame de La Fayette. We know that she was not a believer and that she had, in her own way, returned to ancient wisdom and Stoicism, as her famous novel testifies.[16]

In his essay on *Voluntary Death in Japan*, Maurice Pinguet established a comparison between the spirit of the Japanese sword nobility and that of European aristocracy in its autumn, in the baroque period, between the end of the 16th and beginning of the 17th century. This is worth reflecting on: "While recognizing the same principles of honor and service as the samurai, the sword nobility (French) did not succeed in making its values triumph, for since the failure of the Fronde, it is a bourgeois version of Christian beneficence that asserts itself. It will console itself by mocking pharisaism, by laughing at hypocrites and their dupes." This is, indeed, what La Rochefoucauld and the former Fronde refugees in despair in Jansenism did. "In Japan," continues Pinguet, "martial ethics succeeded in imposing itself because it emphasized abnegation [...] He who answers for his honor with his life cannot be suspected of lying. He acts, that is enough..."[17]

This is not a banal thought. It is even a thought of great altitude, but it corresponds only very indirectly to what Stoicism can inspire in a woman or man of today, whatever their age.

---

16   Claude Dulong, of the Institute, Amoureuses du Grand Siècle (Le Rocher, 1996).

17   Maurice Pinguet, *La Mort volontaire au Japon* (Gallimard, 1984).

CHAPTER VI. OUR HIDDEN WISDOM   163

In substance, towards what behavior does the spirit or school of Stoicism lead as it has evolved down to us? To be Stoic, it is still true, consists in being firm in trials. This is already not bad, but one could add another notion by emphasizing that it also consists in cultivating bearing. Physical bearing and moral bearing. To be quite clear, I am going to allude to a film of great quality, which has rightly enjoyed success. I want to speak of *The Queen* by Stephen Frears (2006), with Helen Mirren in the main role. For one who reflects a little beyond interesting adventures, this film describes a certain mental universe, that of the Queen of England. A universe made of great moral bearing at the price of a well-suggested asceticism. For those who might not have seen this film, the account I am going to give of it suffices to reveal its demonstrative value.

What *The Queen* Reveals

The Queen reconstitutes the drama that shook Great Britain, to the point of endangering the monarchy, during the pitiful week (from Sunday, August 31 to Saturday, September 6, 1997) that followed the accidental death of Lady Di in Paris, until her solemn funeral in Westminster Cathedral. For the queen and her entourage, this death, occurring in rather seedy circumstances, was strictly a private matter. Diana was no longer part of the royal family since she had divorced Prince Charles. One should not give way to emotion. There needed to be dignity and discretion. The children of the broken couple also needed to be protected against media savagery.

In the closed world that protected her, the queen did not imagine the collective hysteria that, like a tornado, would seize public opinion, battered by television as much as by the written press. Seemingly for the first time, a gulf of misunderstanding separated her from her people.

On the other hand, if one believes the film, Tony Blair (Michael Sheen), the recently elected Labour prime minister, understood very quickly that Diana was a formidable pop star with whom the public identified, and from whom advantage should be taken. He perceived the intense emotion of opinion aroused and unleashed by the media. On the first day, he found the words to say of Diana that she was "the people's princess." Unlike the queen, this skillful and calculating politician was in sync with opinion. He immediately thought that public funerals and a televised declaration by the queen would be indispensable to calm opinion. Discreetly supported by Prince Charles, he strove to convince the queen, to win her over to an idea that repelled this woman's modesty and her sense of royal dignity. The film evokes the dramatic moment where the Stoic values of self-discipline, duty and tradition, incarnated by the representative of a millennial monarchic institution, enter into conflict with the emotivity of crowds lost in narcissism.

An Aristocratic Aesthetic

The Queen remarkably displays the crossed evolution of two opposed mentalities which, by the miracle of royal majesty, end up meeting. Tony Blair, initially shocked and paralyzed by the queen's apparent coldness, finally understands that one could not ask this woman, who sacrificed everything for the sake of bearing and the defense of traditions, to jettison these overnight. Conversely, the queen, initially indignant at the sudden sanctification of the little-esteemed Diana, finally admits that she could not remain apart from the popular emotions that were turning to storm.

Against her own entourage, Blair came to defend "this woman who had sacrificed everything for 50 years for a job she had not wanted, without failing once…" This woman whom one sees weep only for an instant in the film, alone and without witness, except for a royal stag that had surged before her on the Scottish moors of Balmoral during a hunt. A poignant and magnificent scene.

Subtly, the spectator is led to perceive that the queen's conduct is not the effect of coldness, but that of sacrifices consented to a function that is a priesthood. He comes to feel respect for the queen's Stoicism, or rather her neo-Stoicism.

That the main character of *The Queen* belongs to the exceptional is evident. This singularity is associated with her function and the demanding idea that inhabits her. But this exceptionality underscores the queen's superior feelings, which are the prerogative neither of her function nor of her rank. The same feelings, less spectacular, certainly inhabit many of her anonymous subjects and many other people elsewhere. Stoicism is not the property of any social category. Not to complain, to keep one's troubles to oneself, not to display one's feelings, moods, states of soul, emotional or gastric dramas. To forbid oneself from speaking of money, health, heart, and sex, quite the contrary of what is spread in hairdressing salon magazines and among "shrinks."

In his novel *The Notebooks of Colonel Bramble*, André Maurois, who had participated in the First World War, traced an eloquent portrait of young British officers raised in the school of Stoicism: "Their youth was spent hardening their skin and heart. They fear neither a punch nor a blow of fate. They consider exaggeration as the worst of vices and coldness as a sign of aristocracy. When they are very unhappy, they put on a mask of humor. When they are very happy, they say nothing at all…" Having no control over destiny, they were taught to control themselves.

The School of Bearing

Constraint, opposed to laxity, has always been the very foundation of childhood education outside periods of decadence. There is no education without prohibitions repeated with constancy and firmness: not to hit one's little sister, not to stick out one's tongue, nor answer with insolence, nor throw mush on one's mama, nor throw tantrums or eat like a pig… Prohibitions that maternal affection compensates.

Through concern for bearing, Stoicism is akin to a sort of aristo-cratic ideal. An ambiguous qualifier, often devalued by the decadence of many former aristocracies. In a brilliant contrarian novel, *The Elegance of the Hedgehog*, Muriel Barbery rehabilitated it by tracing the portrait of a Portuguese cleaning woman, Manuela, friend of Renée, concierge of a Parisian building, which is the novel's setting. This apparently very ordinary woman is in her way an "aristocrat." And of this word, the novelist proposes her definition: "What is an aristocrat? It is a woman whom vulgar does not reach, even though she is surrounded by it."[18]

Let this thought penetrate our mind, then let us add a fundamental remark about Stoicism in order to distance from it the suspicion of insipidity glimpsed by Cioran. It is a matter of recalling its heroic part as illustrated by Cato of Utica, and whose echo is found at all periods among some great passionate persons, those who furnish Corneille's theater for example. One also thinks of the stupefying character of Charlotte Corday, the great-great-granddaughter of the great tragedian.

The reasons for this pretty young woman's action are not to be sought in her noble attachments.[19] She was not at all royalist and had detached herself from religion. She drew her examples from Roman Antiquity and meditating on Plutarch. Initially favorable to the na-scent Revolution, that of the years 1789 and 1790, she distanced herself from it to the point of rebelling with disgust and anger in view of the sectarian and bloody drifts that came afterward. Her indignation and fiery temperament were to lead her — she who was all feminin-ity — with incredible audacity and determination to kill Marat with her own hand, on July 13, 1793. For her, Marat was the incarnation of a horror from which one had to free oneself without hesitating about the price to pay. In the hours that followed her gesture, she faced the

---

18   Muriel Barbery, *L'Élégance du hérisson* (Gallimard, 2006), p. 29.

19   I devoted a study to Charlotte Corday in *La Nouvelle Revue d'Histoire* no. 27 (November 2006).

Revolutionary Tribunal and the guillotine with a firm face, without a moment of weakness.

Cato of Utica and Augustine

Charlotte Corday and Cato of Utica: two incarnations of the "extreme wisdom" of Stoicism in exceptional circumstances.

Nothing really obliged Cato to commit suicide except his pride and dignity. Plutarch suggests that Caesar, his adversary, was open to reconciliation. The period was that of the last great civil war, that which opposed Pompey and Caesar, in whom Cato saw a dangerous demagogue, a future tyrant, the gravedigger of the *mos majorum*, the ensemble of living traditions of Romanity.

Civil wars are horrible, but sometimes conducive to gestures of grandeur. Pompey, beaten at Pharsalus, is assassinated in Egypt. Cato gathers the debris of the army, reaches Tunisia and shuts himself in Utica, a city on the coast near Carthage, populated by Phoenicians reputed to be untrustworthy and crafty. Harboring no illusions about the chances of resisting Caesar, Cato invests himself in getting his partisans to safety. These duties accomplished, one April evening in 46 before our era, after having had dinner with his friends, he has his sword brought to him. He draws it from its sheath and examines it. Plutarch lends him a magnificent word: "Now, I belong to myself." In other words: "Henceforth, I am no longer subject to anything or anyone. I depend only on myself." Cato falls asleep for a moment. "He has his courage, upright, at the side of his bed…"[20] When day breaks, the general awakens. His courage has not weakened. Twice he strikes himself with his sword. People rush to save him from himself. A doctor even sews up the wound. But he reopens the wound and finally dies. In Rome, despite the baseness of the moment, all contemporaries admired Cato for this death, which accomplished the high dignity of his entire life.

---

20 Henry de Montherlant, *Le Treizième César* (Gallimard, 1970).

Yet, there was subsequently found a mind destined for celebrity under the name of St. Augustine to attempt to denigrate Cato's gesture. The height of the great Roman stood as the strongest objection to the moral inversion that the theologian strove to impose in response to the interrogations of his tormented soul, to the requirements of his new religion,[21] and to his desire to shine. Augustine's attempt is recorded in Book I of his famous treatise *The City of God*.

The Fabulous Project of Constantine

I have already evoked the circumstances which, following a series of major and unforeseen historical events toward the end of the 4th century of our era, precipitated the adoption of a cult of Oriental origin as state religion by a Roman Empire turning cosmopolitan.

Such is the historical framework in which *The City of God* was written, more than four and a half centuries after Cato's suicide, it must be emphasized. Augustine wrote his great treatise to respond to the intense emotion provoked by the sack of Rome by Alaric's Visigoths, on August 24, 410. This was an event of more symbolic than political scope. For several years, Emperor Honorius and his administration had been installed in Ravenna. But Rome remained a symbol, the greatest symbol! The fall of Rome was inscribed in a period of troubles opened a century earlier by Constantine's decision to authorize and even favor Christianity through his Edict of Milan (313). This decision had been extended by his successors, notably Emperor Theodosius, who, by the end of several edicts (from 380 to 392), had made Christianity the obligatory religion of the Empire, bringing the Church the support of public power, while the ancient cults were proscribed under threat of death.[22] This immense political

---

21   Brilliant and ambitious, initially Neoplatonic and Manichaean, Augustine only converted to Christianity later, after it had become the state religion and opened access to great intellectual and administrative careers.

22   The adoption of Christianity as state religion implied that all servants of the State, whatever their intimate convictions, had to make an act of submission

and religious revolution clashed with the resistance of some faithful Romans, those whom the Christians called "pagans." The fall of Rome awakened interrogations and criticisms of the effects of Christianity. The new religion was accused of having disarmed Rome and being responsible for the catastrophe. It was to respond to this accusation that Augustine wrote his great treatise. After striving to refute the accusations, he developed at length the idea he had of the new religion. An idea that has not ceased to influence religious debates from century to century.

From *Dignitas* to *Humilitas*

Cato's suicide, a major fact in the moral history of the West, naturally occupied Augustine, for so much did this gesture frontally oppose his own representations. He invoked first of all a rather rudimentary argument borrowed from Platonic logic: "He who kills himself kills nothing other than a man." This was a detour to make suicide a homicide, and therefore a crime. An accusation servilely repeated by jurists throughout Christendom in the Middle Ages and beyond. Understanding that he had to support his demonstration with more subtle arguments, Augustine strove to demonstrate that Cato's suicide

---

which favored their career. This practice had begun before Theodosius' edicts. In his work *Les Divins Césars*, Lucien Jerphagnon cites and comments on the example of Ambrose of Milan (future saint). He was a high imperial official, governor of the province of Liguria-Emilia. He found himself suddenly elected, in 374, to the episcopal seat of the imperial city (Milan) when he was not yet baptized. To make the situation clear, Jerphagnon actualizes it: "One must imagine," he says, "a regional prefect bombarded overnight as the archbishop of Paris, with no other preparation than a little second-year catechism. Except that, in those days, the prefect financially lost nothing, quite the contrary, and even gained in social surface and political influence." And Jerphagnon adds: "Ambrose had transported to the episcopal throne the same authoritarian energy, the same taste for command that he previously deployed in his office." Lucien Jerphagnon, *Les Armes et les mots* (Robert Laffont, "Bouquins", 2012), p. 672. This volume brings together several works by this historian of ancient Rome.

was not the effect of his greatness of soul. It was difficult to deny this, and Augustine did not succeed. It is not only that Cato had refused to bow before Caesar's victory. He had refused to be the witness of a victory that, in his eyes, signified the death of the Roman Republic. It had seemed unthinkable to him to continue living under the power of the man he had personally fought at the highest rank. It would have been even more unworthy to beg for his clemency. And the question of what he should do could only be debated face to face with himself. Of his decision, he was the sole judge. His moral greatness, his *gravitas*, as the Romans said, led him to decide against the pressing advice of his close ones and his own son. Concern for his *dignitas* prevailed over any other consideration, beginning with the desire for life, this ephemeral thing to which humans cling so much.

By acting thus, Cato showed that he was an authentic Roman of old stock, for whom *gravitas*, *virtus*, and *dignitas* were the foundations of behavior. *Gravitas*, the greatness of soul, encompasses the two other notions: *virtus*,[23] moral courage, and *dignitas*, close to what honor would be for the European nobility.[24]

For the *patres* (the patricians, members of the Senate), *dignitas* was the highest good, more important than life. It was not the ideal of all (in the sense of "human dignity"), but that of each one, at his own risk and peril.

This is what Augustine strove to argue against in the name of another moral and religious representation of which he was long the most famous interpreter. With various fortunes, the new religion strove to substitute the believer's *humilitas* for the Roman's *dignitas*. Augustine had not been wrong in targeting Cato, an accomplished example of *dignitas*. All the difficulty came from the fact that they did not speak the same language. How to make Cato enter a schema

---

23 *Virtus*: the specific quality of the *vir* (man in the "virile" sense of the word) which, by phonetic evolution, yielded "virtue."

24 The Latin word *honor* does not have the same meaning as the French "*honneur*" derived from it. It applies to official functions in the *res publica*. On the other hand, *dignitas* can be translated as dignity as well as honor.

of thought that was foreign to him? And yet the stakes were high! If humans, following Cato's example, draw their moral greatness from themselves, without the help of the new religion, how can it justify itself? It was therefore necessary to force Cato into the narrative inaugurated by the founding dogma of "original sin," from which comes the idea of man's sinful and unworthy nature. A dogma from which consequentially proceeds the theology of Salvation. Without original sin, no more Salvation and no more Augustine. So, Cato, this symbol, had to be crushed in order to persuade humans that they were sinners, weak, and unworthy. And, if one believes Augustine and his followers, the more humans were sinners, weak, and unworthy, the closer they were to God, the more they pleased God and his clergy.

Did Augustine's demonstration and all the power acquired by the new religion succeed in convincing Cato's admirers? This is doubtful. Yet, the zeal and dialectical talent of Augustine are not in question. The father of theologians had summated everything in the already cited formula: "Two cities have been formed by two loves: the earthly by the love of self, even to the contempt of God; the heavenly by the love of God, even to the contempt of self." Was Cato driven by self-love in cruelly killing himself with his sword? Augustine's formulation, in this case, seems inadequate. As for contempt for God, this question did not arise for Cato. The Christian God had not yet been revealed when he died. It is certain, on the other hand, that in the manner of all his contemporaries, he respected the gods of his City. He certainly did not care about being "saved" in another world, which was devoid of meaning for him. On the other hand, it mattered to him to behave worthily here and now, face to face with himself, according to the criteria of what is noble or not. Unlike Augustine's God, Cato's divinities had not formulated moral prohibitions. Like his ancestors and like most men, except for some perverts or deranged people devoid of all moral conscience, he found within himself the guide to conduct himself with decency, measure, and benevolence. He was to himself his own director of conscience.

Bossuet's Funeral Orations

Augustine's interpretation was imposed as long as Christianity benefited from the privilege of sacred speech. His pessimistic idea of human nature and his doctrine of predestination of grace knew a revival of influence in France in the 17th century through Jansenism and even beyond. Under Louis XIV, the great preacher that was Bossuet felt certain ideas of this movement without himself being a Jansenist. A large part of his reputation came from the funeral orations which he pronounced in honor of great personages. His art in this domain culminated with that of the Prince of Condé, who was little inclined toward religion.[25] In his orations, the recalling of great actions was always followed by the conclusion that everything in regard to divine greatness and eternal life is an illusion. For the impetuous preacher covered with honors, all human beings were only mud, equal only in abjection. Death revealed this profound equality. Sitting at the edge of the tomb, Bossuet put all his eloquence into beating down the pride and merits of princes and kings who, after having been distinguished for an instant on earth by their exploits, would be forever confounded in common dust. Making death the revelation of fundamental equality incidentally prepared the way for the egalitarian theories of the following century. Inequalities had only been tolerated insofar as they were inscribed in "God's plan" during the brief duration of human life. When it came to eternity, they lost all meaning: "Death confounds the prince and the subject: between them there is only a distinction too fleeting to merit being counted."

Despite this, we continue to admire the ardor and exceptional *coup d'œil* of the Great Condé as well as Turenne's exploits... Yet, the Jansenist slope of the period considered their personal merits to be nothing. In the evangelical doctrine of Salvation, the prodigal son, the lost sheep or the eleventh-hour worker are the object of all attention.

---

25 See notably Simone Bertière's work, *Condé. Le héros fourvoyé* (éditions de Fallois, 2011).

They are even preferred to the exemplary faithful, since God decides who is saved or not. What is shown in this way is the fundamental unworthiness of humans, however great and meritorious they might be according to the criteria of the earthly city. And the prodigal son who returns to God *in extremis* even enjoys a preference that disturbs our sense of justice.

This abolition of the distinction between "the prince and the subject" is an effect of Christianity's egalitarian doctrine and, one is tempted to add, of a secular desire for revenge by ecclesiastical power over that of princes and kings — a revenge in some way of the Altar over the Throne, in this instant of death that authorizes the priest to impose himself on the prince. Take the example of the strange rite to which the Habsburg emperors had consented for their burial in the crypt of the Capuchin Church in Vienna, a rite carried out one last time for the funeral of Empress Zita — the last empress — on April 1, 1989.[26]

Before the church, the master of ceremony stops the procession and strikes the door of the crypt with his silver-knobbed cane. From inside, near the staircase leading to the tombs, a brother porter asks the first question:

- *Who asks to enter?*

The response lists the 53 titles of the deceased.

- *I do not know her.*

A second time, the master of ceremony's cane strikes the door.

- *Who asks permission to enter?*, asks the Capuchin again.

- *Zita, Her Majesty the empress and queen.*

---

26 I borrow the description of this scene from Jean des Cars' book *La Saga des reines* (Perrin, 2012), p. 356. One can specify that Empress Zita only reigned two years (1916–1918), with her husband Emperor Charles, forced to abdicate in November 1918. All testimonies concerning her emphasize both her great piety and a very elevated sense of duty during an existence rendered very difficult by cruel exile.

– I do not know her.

Finally, the master of ceremony strikes a third time.

– Who asks permission to enter?

– Zita, a mortal being, a sinner.

– Let her enter…

Let us leave to each the freedom to appreciate the significance of this ceremony.

Now let us forget the scene just reported and formulate a reflection of a more general order. What we know of the morals and behaviors of the great or the less great during the Christian centuries shows that the moral prescriptions taught by Augustine's emulators did not sensibly modify their real conduct. These prescriptions rarely diminished the proportion of base or wicked actions.[27] On the contrary, they often dressed them in hypocrisy and dissimulation. Conversely, concern for honor and dignity and fear of public shame have often led humans to improve themselves.

A Superior Wisdom

In the more recent period, Dr. Alexis Carrel (1873–1944) was one of those superior minds whose approach was in a certain measure akin to neo-Stoicism. In a certain measure only. Indeed, he did not limit his efforts to achieving individual wisdom. His ambition was to propose rules of conduct intended for all society, which he gathered in his famous work, *Man the Unknown*, initially published in the United States in 1934[28] and which enjoyed extraordinary, worldwide success.

---

27   Murders, plunder, vengeance, adultery, and various cruelties filled the Christian centuries with the same afflicting constancy as other periods.

28   Since its first French edition published by Plon in 1935, the work has been republished many times by its initial publisher; moreover, it was published by Le Livre de Poche in 1963, and by Presses Pocket in 1979 with a preface by Prof. Robert Soupault.

Winning the Nobel Prize in medicine in 1912, Dr. Carrel was an inventive biologist, a virtuoso of surgery, and above all a mind of exceptional stature. Far from confining himself to his discipline, he was interested in everything pertaining to human life envisaged in its physiological, intellectual and moral aspects, all in order to figure out how modern society could be improved. He was a very open and never dogmatic mind who expressed himself with great clarity. The reading and meditation of his principal work have lost nothing of their pertinence.

His fundamental conception of men and life is found condensed in a quotation drawn from *Man the Unknown*. It is as distant from materialist conventions as from spiritualist concepts that separate soul and body. These lines are to be read slowly in order to be penetrated: "The close dependence of the activities of consciousness and physiological activities accords poorly with the classical conception that places the soul in the brain," writes Carrel, "In reality, the entire body seems to be the substratum of mental and spiritual energies. Thought is the daughter of internal secretion glands as well as of the cerebral cortex. The integrity of the organism is indispensable to the manifestations of consciousness. Man thinks, loves, suffers, admires, and prays at once with his brain and with all his organs."

If one reflects for an instant, there is a truly innovative way of perceiving human reality here. Based on what physiological observation reveals when free from all dogma, it reconnects with ancient wisdom anterior to Plato.[29] On Carrel's part, this was a new way of envisaging responses to the challenges of "modern" society, notably through voluntary eugenics.

One finds in Carrel a host of precious observations for reconstructing oneself or educating children. This one, for example, on the benefits of contrasted living conditions: "Man reaches his highest development when he is exposed to bad weather, when he is deprived

---

29 For Plato, "the body is the tomb of the soul." This interpretation was taken up by Christianity.

of sleep and sleeps at length, when his food is sometimes abundant, sometimes rare, when he conquers through effort his shelter and food. He must also exercise his muscles, tire himself and rest, fight, suffer, sometimes be happy, love and hate, have his will alternately tense and relaxed, struggle against his fellows and against himself. He is made for this mode of existence, like the stomach for digesting food. It is in conditions where adaptive processes are exercised intensely that he becomes most virile. We know how physically and morally solid are those who, from childhood, have been subjected to intelligent discipline, who have endured some privations and accommodated themselves to adverse conditions."[30]

Dr. Carrel was a man of his time, a man of the 1930s, haunted, among other things, by the effects of the First World War and the great economic crisis following the crash of 1929. He had an acute perception of the degeneration of the white peoples who had been, for four centuries, the builders of a new type of society associated with the progress of sciences and technology. He was a voluntarist, as one was in his time (before the disasters of the Second World War). He firmly believed in the possibility of curbing the decadence he saw emerging. For this, he thought it necessary to put his conclusions at the disposal of political reformers so that they could make salutary decisions. This elevated ambition stands at the antipodes to rampant individualism, the immediate pleasures promised by the consumption of useless goods, and the compassionate verbiage that dominate our era. But current decadent drifts will only last for a while, like all utopias, including that of communism, the most powerful and murderous of the 20th century. Conversely, Carrel's teachings will retain a constant value.[31]

---

30   *L'Homme cet inconnu*, op. cit., p. 282.

31   In France, Dr. Carrel's personality and thought have been the object of attempts at "demonization" since the 1980s. But this will last only for a while.

THE SPIRIT OF THE *ILIAD*

THIS BREVIARY has been written by a European for Europeans — for Hyperboreans, as Nietzsche would say. Others besides them, from other peoples, other cultures, other civilizations, will certainly be able to read it, but then out of simple intellectual curiosity. Whereas for Europeans, sons of the different peoples of the great Boreal homeland, this book is somewhat that of their particular destiny in the universe. It reflects on the causes of the decline and dormancy of the European soul. It shows the perils of hubris and other toxic flaws. Focusing on a hermeneutics of Homer's poems and the contributions of Stoicism as a wisdom for living, it returns to our most authentic sources.

A Page of History Has Begun to Turn

Of course, a book does not have the power to single-handedly reverse the course of history and the "representations" which seem to be definitively established in minds. A book never has the power to change the world, and it would be ridiculous to hope that it might. It is the world that changes and sometimes awaits new books. We have entered into such changes.

Despite the catastrophes that have made Europe into a cowardly, amnesiac, shapeless, and guilt-ridden ensemble, seeking to protect itself from the violence of the Barbarians through imploring and vile flattery, the revolt against such indignity has begun before our very eyes, often coming from where it was unexpected, tracing out the omens of an interior reconquest. To become master of oneself and in one's own home again, such is the hope. To be able to look at one's children without paling with shame, and, when the day comes, to leave life knowing the heritage is assured.

Before our eyes, a page of history has begun to turn. We have entered an epoch that will know intense upheavals. These will demand new "representations," new visions of the world and new energies. Their premises already arouse the need for Europeans to return to themselves, to the spirit of their spirit. This Breviary has no other objective than to accompany and deepen this need.

Intimately conscious of what I owe essentially to my origins, I wish to say that I justify and will always support the fundamental right of all other humans to possess their own homeland, their own culture, a rootedness that allows them to be themselves, at home, and not to be nothing.

This is also why I rebel against what denies me. I rebel against the programmed invasion of our cities and our countries, I rebel against the negation of French and European memory. I owe to this memory examples of bearing, valor, and refinement hailing from the most distant past, that of Hector and Andromache, of Odysseus and Penelope. Threatened like all my European brothers with perishing spiritually and historically, this memory is my most precious possession. The one on which to rely in order to be reborn.

Men Exist Only Through What Distinguishes Them

Beyond each person's beliefs, there exist fundamental principles of all human life that the confusion of all reference points requires us to recall.

First, as Heidegger brilliantly formulated in *Being and Time* (*Sein und Zeit*), the essence of man is in his existence and not in an "other world." It is here and now that our destiny is played out until the last second. And this ultimate second is as important as the rest of life. It is by deciding for oneself, by truly wanting one's destiny, that one is victorious over nothingness. There is no escape from this requirement since we have only this life, in which it belongs to us to be entirely ourselves or to be nothing. Homer suggested this great truth very well, but, as was his habit, without conceptualizing.

In their diversity, men exist only through what distinguishes them — clans, peoples, nations, cultures, civilizations — and not through what they superficially have in common. Only their animality is universal. Sexuality is common to all humanity as much as the necessity of nourishing oneself. In contrast, each civilization has its singular manner, which belongs to it alone, of ritualizing love, of preparing foods and drinks — arts, gastronomy, customs, etc. proceed from a millennial effort of creation in continuity with itself. Love between two persons of opposite sex as Europeans conceive it, and which courtly love magnified from the 12th century onward, is already present implicitly in the Homeric poems. Even the strong perception of what a person is, the political existence of free cities, as well as the fundamental idea that men are not strangers to nature, that they espouse its cycle of perpetual renewal including birth and death, that finally from the worst can emerge the best — these are all constitutive particularities already present in the founding poems which present us with models for finding ourselves again.

Even when they don't know it, individuals and peoples have a vital need for roots, traditions, and civilizations of their own, that is to say, for reassuring continuities, rites, internalized order, and spirituality. We Europeans hunger for beauty, notably in the small things of life, in true works of art, music, architecture and literature. In other words, these truths of which many peoples remain conscious have often been erased among today's Europeans by the combined effects of Christian universalism and that of the Enlightenment, transposed into the cosmopolitanism of merchant societies. The belief in our

universal vocation is erroneous and dangerous. It is erroneous because it denies other cultures and other civilizations which it would
like to annihilate for the benefit of a supposed world culture of
consumption and "human rights," which are only the rights of mer-
chandise. This belief is dangerous because it locks "Westerners" into
an ethnocentrism that negates other cultures. It forbids them from
recognizing that other men do not feel, do not think, do not live like
them, and that these particularities are legitimate, provided one does
not want to impose them on us.

Having these realities in mind, one can posit as a principle that
there is no universal response to questions of existence and behavior.
Each people, each civilization has its truth and its gods, equally respectable. Each brings its responses, without which individuals, men
or women, deprived of identity, and thus of substance and depth, are
precipitated into bottomless confusion. Like plants, men cannot do
without roots. But their roots are not only those of heredity, to which
one can be unfaithful, but are also those of the spirit, that is to say, of
the tradition that it belongs to each person to reappropriate.

A New Reformation

To think and say these truths constitutes in itself a sort of revolution
of the spirit. But for this to be accomplished, several conditions depend on us. "There would be no need for a very numerous dissident
group to profoundly change modern society. It is a given of observation that discipline gives men great strength. An ascetic and mystical
minority would rapidly acquire irresistible power over the pleasure-
seeking and degraded majority. It would be capable, by persuasion or
by force, of imposing other forms of life on it. No dogma of modern
society is unshakeable."[1]

---

1   Alexis Carrel, *L'Homme cet inconnu* [1935] (Plon, 1968), p. 348. These truths are
     still current.

The rest would follow naturally, up to the conversion of men of power capable of supporting the awakening. One thinks of Emperor Marcus Aurelius, who became a disciple of Epictetus when the latter had died well before his accession.

I wish that in the future, from the bell tower of my village, as well as at those of our cathedrals, one will continue to hear the soothing chiming of bells. But I wish even more that the invocations heard under their vaults change. I wish that one ceases to implore pardon and pity and instead calls for vigor, dignity, and energy. I wish that there will come from within a new Reformation in the spirit of a return to our authentic sources, for which Pope Benedict XVI opened up perspectives in his discourse at Regensburg in 2006. A Reformation that would give full place to the multiple faces of the protective Virgin, Our Lady, the Madonna, already present in the most ancient Antiquity, under the soothing form of the beneficent fairies of the Celtic world or the great figures of Athena or Artemis in ancient Greece.

To those who would turn to pose the eternal question "what is to be done?", I would respond: "Do not expect recipes for action from me." If you feel the desire to act in politics, get involved, but knowing that politics has its own rules, which are not those of ethics.[2] And above all, do not forget my teaching. The upheavals of our time have causes that exceed the forces of politics or social reforms alone. It is not enough to modify laws or to replace one minister with another in order to construct order where chaos reigns. To change behaviors, beginning with those of leaders, one must reform minds, a task always to be begun again and anew. Whatever your action, your priority must be to cultivate in yourself, each day, like an inaugural invocation, an indestructible faith in the permanence of European tradition.

---

2   I devoted several pages to this question in the last chapter of my essay *Le Choc de l'Histoire* (Via Romana, 2011) [*The Shock of History* (Arktos, 2015)], where I develop the notion of the "mystical body" in politics as well as in religion.

I sometimes think of the despair of Symmachus, called "the last Roman."[3] A great Roman aristocrat, Symmachus lived at the end of the 4th century, a sinister epoch among them all. He died as a despairing witness to the end of ancient Romanity. He was unaware that the spirit of Romanity, itself heir to Hellenism, would subsequently be reborn under new forms and that Christianity, under constantly changing aspects, would more often be a "pagano-Christianity" than a "Judeo-Christianity," after nourishing itself on a tradition it had not been able to abolish. He was unaware that the European soul, in other words, the spirit of the *Iliad*, would endure through the centuries, surpassing the succession of generations.

We who know history over thousands of years and scrutinize it with the anxious gaze that could have been Symmachus', we know what he did not know. We know that, individually, we are perishable, but that the spirit of our spirit is indestructible, as is that of all great peoples and all great civilizations. In the present period, it is not only the Europe of politics or of power that has been sleeping since the destructive wars of the 20th century. It is above all the European soul that is in dormancy.

When will the great awakening come? I don't know, but I don't doubt this awakening. I have shown in this Breviary that the spirit of the *Iliad* is like an underground river, inexhaustible and always renewing, which it belongs to us to rediscover. Because this continuity is invisible and yet true, it must be remembered every evening and morning. And in this way, we will be invincible.

For having been thrown down from the dominant position that was still ours before 1914, then plunged into an abyss of negation and guilt, we are the first Europeans to be positioned before the obligation to entirely rethink our identity by returning to our authentic sources. The Antiquity that we invoke is not that of scholars. It is a living Antiquity that we have the task of reinventing. Thus have we

---

3   I evoked the figure of Symmachus in *Histoire et tradition des Européens*, op. cit., pp. 39–41.

undertaken to recompose our tradition, to make of it a creative myth. This cannot be done only through writings and words. The intense effort of refounding must be authenticated by acts of a sacrificial and foundational value.

DOMINIQUE VENNER
completed on the Winter Solstice,
Christmas, 2012

PRACTICAL ADVICE FOR EXISTING AND TRANSMITTING

Practical Advice No. 1

TO BEGIN and build your "inner citadel," take example from the young Berlin woman of 1945 (beginning of chapter 6): regularly keep your own "breviary." Then you will be able to overcome the dereliction caused by the accumulation of readings, one chasing the other and leaving only emptiness. Choose a sewn notebook (rather than spiral-bound), format 17 x 10 (it fits in the pocket) or 20 x 15, 200 pages, small grid. Sober and discreet cover (avoid garish colors and incongruous illustrations). On the first page, carefully write: "Personal breviary, opened on..." Leave this page blank.

Later, when you have collected some illustrations according to your taste, it will be time to choose the one that speaks to you most (the most timeless) in order to paste it. Number the pages by hand from 1 to... Each time you note a reflection, copy (or paste) a quote or text, date them. If you paste a newspaper clipping, naturally note the source and date of the document. Do the same if it's a quote from a book. It is necessary to reference everything precisely from the beginning. This will give value to your later re-readings. Keep the last four pages of the notebook blank to inscribe a thematic index of the collected texts. Hence the usefulness of numbering the pages.

Re-reading one's own "breviary" a few months or years after the first notations brings a feeling of serenity through the rediscovery of the best that one has within oneself. It is also an excellent exercise in observing the evolution of one's feelings, thoughts and judgments.

Practical Advice No. 2

Each day, a few moments of reading. Step back, not to flee the world, but to reconstitute your forces and refuel your energy. Do what Marcus Aurelius did, each evening on campaign, after marching or battle, to write his *Meditations*. Like him, free yourself each day, even for a few minutes, from the constraints imposed by multiple obligations. This naturally applies to the mother of the family, especially one who works outside and must assume so many exhausting tasks (for example going to pick up the children at daycare, at the babysitter's, at school dismissal…) and after having faced public transport. Reclaim a moment for yourself. At home, create a "break" with the outside world: turn off your mobile phone, television, radio, cut the internet connection. Relearn silence in order to find yourself. One quickly discovers its benefit. Also re-read a few pages of one of your favorite novels or essays, without forgetting the notations of your personal "breviary." During your readings, don't hesitate to mark pages and write comments in the margins (date them: one realizes that a few months apart, one interprets a text or reflection differently).

If you are in charge of children, encourage their taste for reading without forcing them. Make books available to them. And let them entertain themselves even with readings that would seem devoid of interest to you. "Serious" readings will come in their time. The important thing is to develop their friendship with books.

Practice reading aloud with children. This will sharpen their pleasure in texts and contribute to weaving a very strong bond between them and you. It's also a way to ward off television or stupid video games.

When you travel, never forget to bring one or two books that are dear to you, novels, essays, varied historical works, memoirs of times past… Thinking about the book that awaits you is already breathing at the end of an exhausting day. A beloved book allows one to isolate oneself from the agitation or ugliness everywhere, in the waiting line of an administration as well as in the crowd of a train station.

Practical Advice No. 3

Whatever your sex, you will benefit from regularly practicing a some-what vigorous sport outdoors or (/and) a combat sport. This will keep you in shape. Moreover, you will discover something important: the ambient decadence does not mean that there is more baseness, stu-pidity, or cowardice than in other eras, it only means that these are what set the tone. In the practice of sports with risk, you will see that energy, courage, and concern for excellence have never totally desert-ed our sick society. These qualities are also present where one does not imagine them, in the invisible strata of professional or family ac-tivities one assumes, in demanding disciplines, such as classical dance or horseback riding. Most often, this natural good health is not ac-companied by any awareness of higher stakes. It has been transmitted within a profession, a family, an artistic or sporting discipline. These are "deposits" of good health in a dilapidated universe. Deposits on which a renaissance can rely.

Practical Advice No. 4

Don't let a week pass without going for a walk in the forest or in nature that is still almost wild, at the very least in an unpolluted urban park. All the regions of France and countless regions of Europe are condu-cive to these retreats in nature, far from the miasmas of the city. You can elect to do a brief walk or a real hike, but the important thing is in the break, the smell of the woods, the soil, the colors, attention to the trees and plants according to the seasons, the possible presence of wild animals whose tranquility you will scrupulously respect. One does not speak in the forest. No shouting. Immersion in splendor, silence, poetry.

If you are in the city for any reason, upon leaving an exhausting work meeting, rather than following the herd of colleagues who are going to have a drink (you can join them later), withdraw for a moment. Ideally in a public garden (without the public) or a church. It is not necessary to be a practicing Christian to enter. The calm, silence, and architectural beauty make a church a beneficial place of retreat. The churches of Europe admirably bear witness to the genius of our peoples, like the ancient temples and so many other monuments. The goal is not to attend a service that could disturb your meditation. Sit apart so as to let yourself be penetrated by the silence that breaks with the triviality of the outside world. In a church, one can naturally read secular texts discreetly.

Practical Advice No. 5

It is good to think and speak of Europe, community of peoples and civilization. It is even better — and even indispensable — to truly live Europe by forming personal ties there, by overcoming routines and linguistic barriers. Via internet and (or) backpack, in the manner of the Wandervögel of yesteryear, set out to meet the boys and girls of our great European homeland. Rediscover the high places of our civilization on the occasion of "pilgrimages" among friends or with family: Stonehenge, Delphi, Brocéliande, Toledo, Alesia, Mont-Saint-Michel, Salzburg, Bayreuth, Sils-Maria… Every pilgrimage implies the effort and pleasure of walking with backpack for several days through beautiful and free nature. Certainly, high places have often become tourist traps. But by playing with dates and schedules, one can nevertheless manage to avoid the crowds. Nothing forbids also creating your own pilgrimage out of the long-distance hiking trails. If they don't all lead to Rome, they will lead to sites that you will have chosen for their beauty, their wildness, their accumulated memories.

Practical Advice No. 6

Cultivate beauty for yourself. Beauty is not a matter of money or consumption. It resides in everything, especially in the small details of life. It is offered freely by nature: the poetry of clouds in a light sky, the crackling of rain on a tent canvas, starry nights, sunsets, first snowflakes, first flowers of the garden, colors of the forest... If the beauty of nature is given to us, that which we dream of in our life requires effort and attention. Remember that there is no beauty (nor joy) without harmony of colors, materials, forms, and styles. This is true for the house, clothes, and small accessories of life. Avoid synthetic materials and plastic in favor of natural materials. There is also no beauty without courtesy in relations with close and less close ones (except boors). Aesthetics founds ethics. There is no beauty without moral and physical bearing. Keep to yourself sorrows and troubles, those of the heart, body, work, or difficult ends of the month. You will gain from being esteemed for your discretion and the pleasure that your company provides.

Practical Advice No. 7

Rediscover the European rites that rhythm the year, notably the traditional calendar festivals associated with the cycles of nature. You will find pleasure in creating your own almanac by systematically noting at their dates the memorable historical memories that you will discover in the course of your readings. Thus, you will have symbols for each day of the year. Another fertile idea would be to compile your own family book, in which you will inscribe information about your direct ancestors, without neglecting photos or old documents. In this book, you will naturally trace a family genealogical tree that you will gradually enrich.

THE REASONS FOR A VOLUNTARY DEATH

I AM SOUND in body and mind, and I am filled with love by my wife and my children. I love life and expect nothing beyond it, except the perpetuation of my race and my spirit. Yet, at the evening of this life, facing immense perils for my French and European homeland, I feel the duty to act while I still have the strength. I believe it necessary to sacrifice myself to break the lethargy that overwhelms us. I offer what remains of my life with an intention of protest and foundation. I choose a highly symbolic place, the Notre-Dame Cathedral of Paris, which I respect and admire, she who was built by the genius of my ancestors on more ancient places of worship, recalling our immemorial origins.

While so many men make themselves slaves to their lives, my gesture embodies an ethic of will. I give myself death in order to awaken slumbering consciences. I rebel against fatality. I rebel against the poisons of the soul and against the invasive individual desires that destroy the anchors of our identity and notably the family, the intimate foundation of our multi-millennial civilization. While I defend the identity of all peoples in their homelands, I also rebel against the crime aimed at the replacement of our populations.

With the dominant discourse incapable of escaping its toxic ambiguities, it falls to Europeans to draw the consequences. Lacking a religion of identity to which we might anchor ourselves, we have a shared memory of our own since the time of Homer, a repository of all the values on which to refound our future renaissance in rupture with the metaphysics of the unlimited, the baneful source of all modern deviations.

I ask forgiveness in advance from all those whom my death will cause to suffer, firstly my wife, my children and grandchildren, as well as my friends and faithful ones. But, once the shock of pain has subsided, I do not doubt that each and all will understand the meaning of my gesture and transcend their grief in pride. I wish that they shall concert together to endure. They will find in my recent writings the prefiguration and explanation of my gesture.

* For any information, one may address my publisher, Pierre-Guillaume de Roux. He was not informed of my decision, but has known me for a long time.

DOMINIQUE VENNER

EULOGY

BY ALAIN DE BENOIST

66 HELLO, FRIEND. You are Fabrice, right?" It was October 9, 1962, and I was not yet 19. Since the previous year, I had been involved with the Federation of Nationalist Students (*Fédération des étudiants nationalistes*, FEN), founded by François d'Orcival at the request of the underground leadership of the Young Nation (*Jeune Nation*) movement. My friends then knew me only as Fabrice Laroche. I was in charge of staffing a rundown office on Rue de la Glacière, where the FEN's general secretariat operated in semi-darkness, and where the basement hosted a cramped meeting room. The man standing before me was slender, of average height, with closely cropped hair and a slight smile. Once I confirmed my identity, he introduced himself: "Dominique Venner" (he pronounced it the Italian way, separating the double consonants: "Ven-ner"). He had just been released from prison, where he had been sent for political activities, including the "reconstitution of a dissolved league" and, more broadly, a kind of sympathetic illegality. (At the end of his trial on June 19, 1963, he was ultimately sentenced to three years' suspended imprisonment). I trace the beginning of a friendship that would last over half a century to that first encounter.

Throughout his time in prison — then commonly referred to among activists as being "*embastillé*" — Dominique Venner remained far from idle. He used his forced stillness to complete his education, reflect on the situation, convert many of his fellow inmates to his ideas, and write several foundational texts, among them the influential *Pour une critique positive* (*For a Positive Critique*), written in July 1962 at Santé prison, which would have a decisive impact on many of us.

He had many plans, beginning with launching a journal. That journal was *Europe-Action*, whose first issue appeared in January 1963. The following year, it transitioned into a monthly illustrated magazine, with Jean Mabire — formerly of *L'Esprit public* — soon taking over as editor-in-chief. Initially based on Rue aux Ours in the Halles district, the offices later moved to the corner of Rue Cassette and Rue de Vaugirard. There was also a publishing house, Éditions Saint-Just, which scandalized conservative circles (Dominique published his first book, *Le procès Vanuxem*, there under the pseudonym Jean Gauvin), and a bookstore, Librairie de l'Amitié, run by Suzanne Gingembre. A whole activist network formed around *Europe-Action*, which FEN promptly joined — without surrendering its autonomy, since it continued to publish its own journal, *Cahiers universitaires*. When, at the end of 1963, the revolutionary, novel, and "Europeanist" ideas of *Europe-Action* caused a break with Pierre Sidos, who clung to a French-centered nationalism, nearly the entire Movement — the term was indeed spoken and written with a capital "M"! *Mouvement!* — joined Venner's line.

In *Mémoire vive*, the memoir I published in 2012 with Bernard de Fallois, I recounted at length the *Europe-Action* adventure — ultimately rather brief, as it lasted barely five years, but one that left a lasting impression. I won't revisit that here, except to reiterate that Dominique Venner was throughout that time its unwavering, friendly, and inspired leader. From the start, we were won over by his demeanor, his manner of speaking, his analytical precision, the thoughtfulness of his directives, and the unshakeable strength of his convictions. Our nearly unconditional admiration for him was never a "cult of the leader," especially since Dominique never presented himself as such, rather only as one militant among others. We simply saw him as the foremost of the revolutionary militants we aspired to be, leaving the taste for personalities and petty chiefs to the "nationals," whom we despised and regarded as no more than chickens to be plucked.

Yet, between the FEN students and the *Europe-Action* support committees, a full fusion never materialized. After two years — 1963 and 1964 — of consuming activism (one might rather say total activism), differences in direction began to emerge between those around Dominique Venner, who wanted to engage further in politics, and others like myself, already inclined toward more "cultural" work. In late May 1965, Dominique rejected my proposal to replace FEN with an Institute of Doctrinal Studies, with *Cahiers universitaires* as its revised publication. He likewise opposed various initiatives of an informal circle I named the *Groupe d'études doctrinales* (GED), arguably a precursor of the *Groupement de recherche et d'études pour la civilisation européenne* (GRECE), the intellectual movement later known as the "*Nouvelle Droite*" ("New Right") starting around 1979. It was at this time that *Cahiers universitaires* shifted towards a new, "metapolitical" series (with issues on cinema, war, fantasy, the North, etc.).

Conversely, the *Mouvement* rushed headlong into political escalation, which proved fatal. By late 1965, *Europe-Action* support committees had been turned into a political movement: the Nationalist Movement of Progress (*Mouvement nationaliste du progrès*, MNP), whose founding congress took place in Paris on April 30, 1966. In November 1966, the MNP became a political party, the European Rally of Freedom (*Rassemblement européen de la liberté*, REL). The "relists" (a nod to "realism") dove into electoral battles only to suffer a crushing defeat in the March 1967 legislative elections. This caused a financial crisis that dismantled the *Mouvement*'s infrastructure and led to *Europe-Action*'s demise. Disputes between the "politicals" and the advocates of doctrinal work deepened, with strong tensions surfacing between Dominique Venner, Jean Mabire, Pierre Bousquet, Robert Desroches, and Maurice Gingembre.

On July 2, 1967, at a heated meeting held at Rue Jean Colly in a condemned building turned into a kind of communal phalanstery,

Dominique Venner solemnly announced he was leaving politics for good. I was there. He later wrote in 2006: "Deeply engaged in partisan action in my youth, I definitively moved away from it. It taught me a lot. I came to see myself as a rebellious heart, rebelling out of loyalty to the upright values of my childhood." Three weeks later, he left France for a short stay in the United States. He later told me of the despair that haunted him then. As I wrote in *Mémoire vive*, his decision — which I fully supported — was a relief to me. Without it, I likely wouldn't have felt free to redirect my own life, which I did at the end of 1967 by launching the journal *Nouvelle École* and taking a lead role in founding GRECE.

Contrary to what has often been said or written, Dominique Venner was never among the founders of what would later become the Nouvelle Droite. In 1968–1969, he remained quite skeptical about the value of focusing solely on the realm of ideas, though he nonetheless sent us a message wishing us good luck. In 1969, he founded and ran the Institute of Occidental Studies (*Institut d'études occidentales*, IEO), for which he sought and obtained the patronage of Thierry Maulnier. The IEO organized a few conferences (I spoke at one of them) and published a journal, *Cité-Liberté*, edited by Jean-Claude Bardet, which only ran for seven issues. The institute disappeared by 1971.

From that point on, Dominique Venner began a completely different career. He didn't change his personality, but added new dimensions to it. Having once dreamed of a military career in his youth but forced to abandon it, he began writing extensively about weapons — a fairly classic "transfer." Over the years, his writing style became increasingly distinguished, and he established himself as an expert on weaponry, as well as on hunting, which he practiced intensively. He also began writing history books, starting with *Baltikum: The Freikorps in the Baltics*, published in 1974 by Robert Laffont. Many more works would follow, as is well known.

During the three decades or so when Dominique withdrew from public life, I remained in close contact with him. I remember with amusement that he lived in my Paris apartment during the May 1968 events. Four years later, on June 21, 1972, he attended my wedding in Hamburg, a wedding that owed him a great deal, indirectly, since I had met my future wife at his home. She was a childhood friend of his first wife, Angelika, a young German woman he had married on December 21, 1965. He followed the development of the Nouvelle Droite closely, read our publications carefully, and occasionally contributed to them. We dined together four or five times a year. In 1997, knowing of his admiration for Ernst Jünger — to whom he would later dedicate a book: *Ernst Jünger: A Different European Destiny*[1] — I dedicated my own essay on Jünger to him.

Having evolved differently, we didn't always agree. More "right-wing" than I was, Dominique remained attached to issues I had personally left behind. Moreover, like many on the right, he didn't hold intellectuals in particularly high regard! From 1966 onward, when de Gaulle withdrew France from NATO's integrated command, I felt increasingly "Gaullist" — in the spirit of Jean Cau, Dominique de Roux, or Jean Parvulesco — whereas he remained consistently hostile to de Gaulle, for reasons not solely related to the Algerian War. When he published *De Gaulle: Grandeur and Nothingness* (Rocher, 2004), it gave us an opportunity to engage in a friendly debate on the pages of *Éléments* (Spring and Summer 2005). That same year, again in *Éléments* (Winter 2005), we also confronted each other somewhat sharply — though always amicably — on what to think of today's right.

Historical reflection ultimately took precedence for Dominique Venner, completing the transformation of the former activist into a "meditative historian," a term he often used to describe himself. His leadership of the journal *Enquête sur l'histoire*, published by the press group behind *Minute*, and later *La Nouvelle Revue d'histoire* (from 2002), allowed him to reconnect with a more "political" audience than

---

1   Dominique Venner, *Ernst Jünger. Un autre destin européen* (Rocher, 2005); in English: *Ernst Jünger: A Different European Destiny*, trans. Roger Adwan (London: Arktos, 2024).

that of his books on hunting or weapons. Starting also in 2002, with the publication of *Histoire et tradition des Européens*, he increasingly took public stances on current events and major contemporary debates. This is likely the version of Dominique Venner that most people today remember.

Since his tragic death in the Notre-Dame on May 21, 2013, Dominique Venner's figure seems to me to have taken on a mythical dimension, in the best sense of the word. Even though most of his life unfolded away from political engagement, many young people today see themselves in him. I'm not surprised — he always wanted to be a rebel. In his most personal book, *Rebel Heart* (*Le cœur rebelle*, 1994), Dominique wrote that "to be a rebel is to be one's own standard. To stick to oneself, no matter the cost. To never recover from one's youth. To rather make enemies than grovel… In defeat, never question the worth of a lost cause." These lines should not be misinterpreted. "To be one's own standard" doesn't mean to arrogantly see oneself as the center of the universe, and even less to justify individualism. It means staying true to what one set out to be — in other words, not betraying oneself. "*Tenue*," bearing or poise, is an ethical matter, a question of style. For Dominique, who valued "*tenue*" above all, style was expressed in simple principles: live and die standing. Do not seek personal interest. Do not scheme, do not evade, do not complain. Do not explain oneself. And also: stay away from gossip, idle talk, or petty chatter. Move toward what uplifts, flee what degrades. His "mentors in bearing" were men and women whose driving force was a sense of honor. Behind that lay an entire worldview. It explains his boundless admiration for the heroes of Homeric epics, which he saw as the founding texts of European tradition.

Because Venner didn't flaunt himself, all of this was only visible to those who knew him best. Others saw in him a reserved man, sometimes even dogmatic. And it's true that he sometimes seemed rigid. In over 50 years, I never saw him laugh heartily! We never used the informal "*tu*" with each other either. For him, "*tenue*" went hand in hand with restraint.

Dominique Venner despised cheats, advisors who never act, and those who demand from others what they themselves cannot live up to. He was interested in ideas, but, as I've said, he wasn't an intellectual. He preferred those who set examples to those who give lessons — he left behind less a doctrine than an example of personal bearing. So much so that he struggled to fully admire a great writer whose daily conduct he found petty. Since I tend to separate life and work — appreciating a work's quality regardless of its author's personality — we had more than one passionate argument on this topic.

Dominique was convinced that Europe would one day awaken from its "slumber." Unlike many we knew, he rejected pessimism and even more so fatalism. In this respect, he was as far removed from the ideology of progress (the Enlightenment) as he was from that of decline (Spengler or Evola). The key lesson from his historical reflections was that history is always open. History is unpredictable, he often said. To tease him, I'd point out that if history is unpredictable, it can also bring the worst...

I remember that during the *Europe-Action* era, Dominique strongly condemned suicide, which surprised me greatly. He saw it as an escape from life. On that point, he changed, becoming an admirer of voluntary death, as were so many ancient Romans. The writings he produced in the years before his death leave no doubt: he constantly had in mind the examples of Mishima, Montherlant, and others. Since we must all depart one day, he would say, it's the ultimate freedom to choose the moment oneself. That's why, like his other close friends, I wasn't surprised by his suicide — only by the date and location. What is certain is that his death aligned perfectly with his life: being far from despair or cowardice. Dominique said so himself when explaining his decision to sacrifice himself "to break the torpor that oppresses us," offering what remained of his life "in a gesture of protest and foundation." In that phrase, "foundation" is clearly the key word. Just hours earlier, he had written: "We are entering a time when words must be validated by deeds."

On January 11, 2013, Dominique Venner gave the eulogy at Père-Lachaise cemetery for his old friend Ferdinand Ferrand, who had died a few days earlier. By then, he likely already knew that not long after, his own eulogy would be spoken in that very same place. Thinking of the words he used that day, I can imagine what he must have been feeling.

I am among the few people who, after Dominique's death, received a letter from him, mailed just hours before he took his own life. He wanted to express to me the importance our friendship had held for him. Recognizing his neat, consistent handwriting on the envelope — unchanging throughout his life — my heart was suddenly crushed with emotion. Breathless, I felt a sob coming. Then I imagined Dominique. "Come on now, Fabrice, pull yourself together." So I did not cry.

ALAIN DE BENOIST

A BRIEF BIOGRAPHY
OF THE AUTHOR

DOMINIQUE VENNER was a writer and historian. He published some 50 works and directed several historical collections. Until his death, he was the director of *La Nouvelle Revue d'Histoire* (NRH) which he founded in 2002. His life shaped his vocation.

Among all his books, there are three that constitute successive milestones for understanding his journey: *Le Cœur rebelle* (*The Rebel Heart*), the *Dictionnaire amoureux de la Chasse* (*Dictionary of Love for Hunting*), and *Le Siècle de 1914* (*The Century of 1914*), to which must be added *Histoire et tradition des Européens* (*History and Tradition of Europeans*) which stands out.

Dominique Venner was born in Paris on April 16, 1935; he had five children. Like Jacques Bainville or Benoist-Méchin before him, he came to the study of history through critical observation of the present. After his secondary education and before studying the history of art and weapons, he enlisted in the army on his 18th birthday (military school of Rouffach). Volunteering later for Algeria, he participated until October 1956, in his own words, in this "little medieval war," which counted greatly in his formation, leading him for about ten years into intense political commitments and the editing of the review *Europe-Action*. Recalling this period, he would say: "Without the radical militancy of my youth, without the hopes, disappointments, failed plots, prison, failures, without this exciting and cruel experience, I would never have become the meditative historian that I am. It is total immersion in action, with its most sordid and most noble aspects, that forged me and made me understand and think about history from the inside, like an initiate and not like a scholar obsessed with insignificances or like a spectator duped by appearances." Dominique Venner recounted these formative years in *Le Cœur rebelle* (Les Belles Lettres, 1994).

Around 1970, he definitively broke with political commitments, which, he would say, did not correspond to his vocation. He even left Paris in order to reconnect with nature, to be closer to the forests and henceforth live by his pen. Year after year, he published a large number of books and collaborated with the press, studying during this first period the little-explored history of weapons and hunting. This epoch of his existence would one day be closed by the publication of the *Dictionnaire amoureux de la chasse* (Plon, 2000), notably acclaimed by Michel Déon.

In parallel, Dominique Venner became involved in publishing activity. Shortly after 1970, André Balland entrusted him with the direction of a collection of historical narratives that would exhibit new authors. Simultaneously, he undertook research on contemporary history in order to answer his own questions. This work led to the publication of *Baltikum* (Robert Laffont, 1974), devoted to the German Freikorps of the years 1919–1923. Later, he would take up this work which, modified and expanded, became *Histoire d'un fascisme allemand, 1919–1934* (*History of a German Fascism, 1919–1934*) (Pygmalion, 1996; 2002), enriched notably thanks to the insights that Ernst Jünger contributed.

Many other historical works would follow, among others *Le Blanc Soleil des vaincus* (*The White Sun of the Vanquished*) (La Table Ronde, 1975), devoted to the American Civil War; *Histoire de l'Armée rouge* (*History of the Red Army*) (Plon, 1981), honored with a prize from the French Academy; *Gettysburg* (Le Rocher, 1995); *Histoire critique de la Résistance* (*Critical History of the Resistance*) (Pygmalion, 1995; 2002); *Les Blancs et les Rouges, Histoire de la guerre civile russe* (*The Whites and the Reds, History of the Russian Civil War*) (Pygmalion,

1997, reprinted and expanded at Le Rocher in 2007); *Histoire de la Collaboration* (*History of Collaboration*) (Pygmalion, 2000; 2002); *Histoire du terrorisme* (*History of Terrorism*) (Pygmalion, 2002); *De Gaulle, la grandeur et le néant* (*De Gaulle: Grandeur and Nothingness*) (Le Rocher, 2004); *Le Siècle de 1914* (*The Century of 1914*) (Pygmalion, 2006). This last work constitutes the third major milestone in his journey, to which must be added his essay *Ernst Jünger. Un autre destin européen* (*Ernst Jünger: A Different European Destiny*) (Le Rocher, 2009), as well as *L'Imprévu dans l'Histoire. Treize meurtres exemplaires* (*The Unexpected in History: Thirteen Exemplary Murders*) (éditions Pierre-Guillaume de Roux, 2012).

Parallel to his work on contemporary history, Dominique Venner published in 2002 *Histoire et tradition des Européens. 30,000 ans d'identité* (*The History and Tradition of Europeans: 30,000 Years of Identity*) (Le Rocher; new edition 2004), a foundational work that questions the sources and destiny of European civilization starting with Homer.

After directing the journal *Enquête sur l'histoire* (*Investigation into History*) from 1991–1999, he founded in 2002, with the support of François-Georges Dreyfus, Philippe Masson, Bernard Lugan and Philippe Conrad, *La Nouvelle Revue d'Histoire* (*The New Review of History*), which proved innovative in both substance and form: "We wanted to found a journal that would put an end to partial and biased interpretations of history, that would sketch another vision of the past and future, that aspired to a European renaissance. We wanted this journal to be modern and aesthetic. Our implicit charter included respect for the philosophical diversity of collaborators, but one and the same attachment to historical honesty without prejudices, the concern finally to express ourselves in a lively, elegant, and clear way for the pleasure of our readers."

To a reader who questioned him about his "optimistic" vision of the future, Dominique Venner offered this response: "My 'optimism,' as you say, is not naive. I do not belong to a parish where one believes that everything ends up working out. I see perfectly well all that is dark in our epoch. I sense, however, that the powers that weigh negatively on the fate of Europeans will be undermined by the historical shocks to come. To achieve an authentic awakening, it will still be necessary for Europeans to be able to reconquer their indigenous consciousness and the long memory of which they have been dispossessed. The trials that come will help us by freeing us from what has deeply polluted us. This is the bold task to which I have devoted myself. It has few precedents and is in no way political. Beyond my mortal person, I have the certainty that the torches lit will not be extinguished."[1]

Commenting on his book *Le Choc de l'Histoire* (Via Romana, 2011) [*The Shock of History* (Arktos, 2015)], interpreting as a sort of intellectual testament and a synthesis of his work,[2] the magazine *Le Spectacle du monde* writes: "Dominique Venner patiently builds, stone by stone, one of the most original works devoted, for a good part, to the European twentieth century envisaged in the long term, brought into relation with the most distant past of the Old Continent, its longest memory, its deep tradition, extracting through its titles a reflection on the destiny of Europe and Europeans."

The testament book of Dominique Venner, *Samouraï d'Occident — Samurai of the West* — was published by Pierre-Guillaume de Roux in 2013. The philosopher Alain de Benoist comments: "This 'breviary' is neither a little catechism nor a recipe book (even if the author offers some advice 'for living and transmitting'). It is more like a compass. It is also an outstretched hand to lead us to the peaks, where the air is crisper, where forms become clearer, where panoramas reveal themselves and stakes become visible. It is an invitation to become who we are. And it is once again from Homer's work — of whom the Ancients said he was "the beginning,

---

1   *La Nouvelle Revue d'Histoire* no. 58 (January 2012).

2   *Le Choc de l'Histoire* [*The Shock of History*] consists of a series of interviews with journalist Pauline Lecomte.

the middle, and the end" — that Dominique Venner draws this triad, which resounds like a directive: 'Nature as foundation, excellence as goal, beauty as horizon.'"

The complete collection of Dominique Venner's editorials published in *Enquête sur l'histoire* and *La Nouvelle Revue d'Histoire* has been gathered in the book *Grandeur et décadences de l'Europe* (*The Grandeur and Decadences of Europe*), published by Via Romana editions in 2021.

Over some 40 years, Dominique Venner wrote dozens of notebooks of notes, returning to his entire life and delivering his personal reflections on numerous subjects. They are currently being published by La Nouvelle Librairie.

OTHER BOOKS PUBLISHED BY ARKTOS

OTHER BOOKS PUBLISHED BY ARKTOS

	Notes on the Third Reich
	Pagan Imperialism
	Recognitions
	A Traditionalist Confronts Fascism
GUILLAUME FAYE	*Archeofuturism*
	Archeofuturism 2.0
	The Colonisation of Europe
	Convergence of Catastrophes
	Ethnic Apocalypse
	A Global Coup
	Prelude to War
	Sex and Deviance
	Understanding Islam
	Why We Fight
DANIEL S. FORREST	*Suprahumanism*
ANDREW FRASER	*Dissident Dispatches*
	Reinventing Aristocracy in the Age of Woke Capital
	The WASP Question
GÉNÉRATION IDENTITAIRE	*We are Generation Identity*
PETER GOODCHILD	*The Taxi Driver from Baghdad*
	The Western Path
PAUL GOTTFRIED	*War and Democracy*
PETR HAMPL	*Breached Enclosure*
PORUS HOMI HAVEWALA	*The Saga of the Aryan Race*
CONSTANTIN VON HOFFMEISTER	*Esoteric Trumpism*
	MULTIPOLARITY!
RICHARD HOUCK	*Liberalism Unmasked*
A. J. ILLINGWORTH	*Political Justice*
INSTITUT ILIADE	*For a European Awakening*
	Guardians of Heritage
ALEXANDER JACOB	*De Naturae Natura*
JASON REZA JORJANI	*Artemis Unveiled*
	Closer Encounters
	Erosophia
	Faustian Futurist
	Iranian Leviathan
	Lovers of Sophia
	Metapolemos
	Novel Folklore
	Philosophy of the Future
	Prometheism
	Promethean Pirate
	Prometheus and Atlas
	Psychotron
	Uber Man
	World State of Emergency
HENRIK JONASSON	*Sigmund*
EDGAR JULIUS JUNG	*The Significance of the German Revolution*
RUUBEN KAALEP & AUGUST MEISTER	*Rebirth of Europe*
LANCE KENNEDY	*The Book of the Scribe*
JAMES KIRKPATRICK	*Conservatism Inc.*
LUDWIG KLAGES	*The Biocentric Worldview*

OTHER BOOKS PUBLISHED BY ARKTOS

www.ingramcontent.com/pod-product-compliance
Lightning Source LLC
Chambersburg PA
CBHW021358090426
42742CB00009B/910